HOW TO GET MORE DONE

First published in Great Britain in 1990 by Kogan Page Limited,
120 Pentonville Road, London N1 9JN.

British Library Cataloguing in Publication Data
A CIP record for this book is available from the British Library.

ISBN 0–7494–0191–5

Typeset by The Castlefield Press Ltd, Wellingborough, Northants.
Printed and bound in Great Britain by Biddles Ltd, Guildford.

Contents

Introduction   7

1 **What Are the Benefits?**   9
Personal productivity 9; Personal objectives 13

2 **What Is Personal Productivity?**   16
Productivity 16; Factors affecting productivity 19;
Personal productivity 19; Resources 22; Points to
remember 24

3 **Making the Most of Your Time**   25
Time 'management' 25; Idle time 28; Wasted time
29; Points to remember 39

4 **Planning Your Strategy**   40
Where to start 41; Setting clear objectives 42;
Planning made easy 44; Personal time 47;
Commuting/Travelling 49; Family and leisure
time 50; Points to remember 52

5 **Getting Help**   53
Organising 53; The 4 Rights 55; Delegation 56;
Management by objective 60; Points to remember
62

6 **Maintaining Progress**   64
Communicating in theory 64; Improving your own
communication 65; Listening 70; Body language
71; Making meetings work 72; Points to
remember 76

7   **Putting Your Plan Into Action**   77
    Avoiding hi-intrusion at the office 77; Avoiding hi-
    intrusion at home 80; Managing your telephone
    81; Getting away from it all 83; Getting it right
    first time 83; Points to remember 85

8   **Self-Assessment**   87
    Utilisation of materials 87; Utilisation of
    machinery 89; Personal resources 90; Points to
    remember 94

9   **Money is the Root . . .**   96
    What is money? 96; Fixed-base budgeting 98;
    Zero-base budgeting 99; Matching income and
    expenditure 102; Increasing income and
    decreasing expenditure 104; Points to remember
    107

10 **Where Do We Go From Here?**   108
    Personal audit 108; Your action plan 109;
    Resources 110; Don't forget the money 110;
    Review your plan 110; Where do we go from here?
    111; Points to remember 111

Index   112

Introduction

Every one of us has potential which is usually only partially realised. There are many reasons why we don't realise our full potential – luck, ill-health, accidents, the actions of others. But the most common reason is our almost universal failure to develop our personal productivity to its maximum.

Most of us think of productivity as something that goes on in factories or businesses and is therefore of little general interest. In fact, productivity is something which greatly affects all of us in both our business and personal lives. Knowing how to measure and improve your personal productivity is to be able to take charge of your life and start to direct it the way you want it to go.

So think of this as a guidebook rather than a textbook and work along with us in easy stages towards your ultimate goal – whatever it may be – making full use of all your potential at last.

Chapter 1
What Are the Benefits?

Whenever someone tries to sell you anything – an insurance policy, a new car, a stereo, or even a 'how-to' book like this – the first and most material thing you want to know is what benefit you can expect to get out of it.

If we were selling you a tangible product – like a stereo – it would be fairly easy to explain in some detail how you would benefit from acquiring it. But what we are selling you is not tangible – or at least not until it has been converted into real terms. Also how much you benefit will depend very much on the present level of your personal productivity.

So, let's answer your question, like all good sales people do, by asking you one. *What is your present productivity compared with your personal potential?*

Personal productivity

Unless you are familiar with productivity and are used to measuring it you will find that quite difficult to answer. To make it easy, just mark the following questions in the Assessment of Personal Productivity (honestly please) using the guide at the top of the form.

Assessment of Personal Productivity	
5 = Always 4 = Frequently 3 = Sometimes 2 = Seldom 1 = Never	
Questions	**Marks**
1. I get 7 hours' sleep a night. 2. I spend 3 hours a day on personal needs (eating, toilet).	

Questions	Marks
3. I spend at least 3 hours a day with my family/friends.	
4. I use 1 hour a day for personal development.	
5. I spend not more than 2 hours per day travelling.	
6. I spend not more than 2 hours a day in meetings.	
7. I spend not more than 1 hour a day on the phone.	
8. I suffer not more than 1 hour of interruptions a day.	
9. I spend not more than 1 hour a day dealing with crises.	
10. I return all calls the same day.	
11. I reply to all mail within 24 hours.	
12. I do nothing that my subordinates could do if I let them.	
13. I read at least 1 educational book a month.	
14. I plan my day every day.	
15. I plan my week every week.	
16. I ensure that all my subordinates have clear objectives.	
17. I prioritise the work I have to do and stick to it.	
18. I spend at least 10 per cent of my time in planning.	
19. I use a tape recorder or machine for dictation.	
20. I actively look for better ways of doing things.	
	%

If you scored more than 80 per cent your personal productivity is unusually high and the only reason you are reading this book is because you won't be satisfied until you get to 100 per cent.

If you scored less than 80 per cent this book will help you to improve your personal productivity and, in addition, will help you to:

- Make more effective use of your time
- Reduce your personal stress
- Improve your working relationships
- Improve your personal life
- Enhance your prospects for promotion

These are fairly big claims. How can we be sure that we can deliver the goods? There we have a problem. We can deliver but we can't guarantee you'll receive.

Over the years, at seminars, workshops, business meetings and social gatherings, we have talked to several thousands of people about their personal productivity – students, employees, managers, academia, housewives. Like you, we have heard the constantly repeated plaints – 'If only I had two pairs of hands.' 'If only there were more hours in a day.' 'If only I had more time.' 'If only . . . '

Yes indeed, 'if only' we didn't have any problems we could all relax on a south sea island, lying around in the sun waiting for the coconuts to drop and feed us. Unfortunately, most of us do have problems and our resources for tackling them are limited. We have only one pair of hands. We have only 24 hours in a day. We have our brain into which has been programmed our learning from education and experience. And we have our bodies complete with whatever disabilities we have collected over the years. Our resources are indeed finite; it is the way we employ them, our *personal productivity*, that determines what we can achieve.

Among all the 'if onlys' there were an outstanding few who used their resources to achieve the goals they had set themselves – learning a language, running a youth group, managing a business empire, bringing up a family or whatever. The actual goals varied but the methods used to achieve them were remarkably similar and boiled down to maintaining personal productivity at the highest possible level.

Generally speaking these people seemed able to do this without working any 'harder' than the others; in fact, in many cases, they appeared to be more relaxed and free of stress than their colleagues and friends. It's one of the many misconceptions about productivity that increasing it means working harder. In most cases (unless you have been loafing) it doesn't mean working harder but working 'smarter' – using your brain instead of your muscles.

One thing they did have in common was *resolution*. Having decided on a goal and planned a way of achieving it, they did not allow themselves to be side-tracked but kept at it until they had succeeded. These people had learned how to do this the hard way – by experience.

There is nothing difficult or complicated about the methods they used. They are easy to understand and to install. The only thing they do require of you is the willingness to try them, and once they have proven useful, the resolution to keep them going.

This book is a summary of those methods and we can promise that you will enjoy all the benefits of improved personal productivity that we have listed, 'if only' you will try to apply them to your life. If you do you may not necessarily spend the rest of your life on an island beach but you will certainly enjoy the great satisfaction of achieving a good deal more than you do at present.

I thought the doctor was unnecessarily rude. 'If you want to live another 10 years,' he growled, 'you'd better do something about your health. You're a real mess – overweight, unfit – you're allowing your life style to kill you.'

'So what do you want me to do?' I asked sullenly. 'You know the hours I have to work.' 'Eat properly and take regular exercise. Here,' he grunted, tossing a couple of leaflets on the desk in front of me, 'here's a diet that won't kill you and some exercises you can do in 10 minutes every day. Come and see me in three months time and we'll see how you shape up then.'

When I got home I read both booklets. The diet recommended daily weighing and gave a reducing scale I should aim for. The exercises were progressive, starting off with just a few press-ups and running on the spot and slowly working up to more energetic exercises.

'I'll show him,' I said to myself and started the diet and the exercises right then. In each case I had two goals to work towards – a long-term goal of making the doctor eat his words and a short-term goal set by the programmes each week.

At the end of the first week I had consumed more salad than I had eaten in the previous three months but I hadn't lost any weight. I was so stiff that keeping up the exercises was a real triumph of mind over rebellious matter. However, I was determined to show that doctor and stuck it out.

Three weeks into the course I started to see results and by the fourth week I was on target with the reducing cycle I had chosen and beginning to feel quite proud of myself.

When I saw the doctor he grudgingly admitted that I had improved a lot, 'But you've still a way to go,' he added.
Some people are never satisfied.

Before we start to explain personal productivity and how improving it will help you to achieve your goals more easily, you have to be certain what you want to achieve – what your goals are – so that you can measure your progress towards them.

Personal objectives

Goals, or personal objectives, are statements of measurable events we want to see happen. For example, a short-term objective at work might be – 'My sales to exceed quota by 10 per cent by the end of the year.' Similarly, a long-term objective might be – 'Appointed marketing director of this company within five years.' Both objectives state a measurable event to be achieved by a certain time. Both will require considerable application of our resources if they are to be achieved.

Setting out your personal objectives in this way is a vital first step towards planning to achieve them and until it is done you are in danger of misapplying your resources. Since these are limited and finite any misuse will detract from your ability to achieve your objectives.

The second step is to improve your personal productivity so that you can use your resources to the full. Measuring your progress towards your objectives will tell you how well you have been able to do this.

So it's worthwhile, before we go any further, for you to take a little time to clarify your own thinking by writing down your personal objectives so that you know what you are aiming for.

When you write them try to state them as events rather than activities – reaching a peak rather than climbing a mountain – because it's easier to measure progress against events.

Try to be honest with yourself. If you want nothing else than to be the next chairman of the board, that's fine. If you would rather spend more time with your family, that's fine too. It's entirely up to you to determine your life's values. However, it might be as well if you wrote them in pencil to start with – you might want to revise them as you get further into this book!

Start with your objectives at work – those connected with your chosen career or job. Some of these will be the objectives of your position as agreed with your boss; others will be of your own choosing and of a more personal nature. If you are working at home bringing up a family you will have many things you want to achieve in that role.

Your objectives at home may be a bit harder to define but are none the less important. Your relationships with family and friends, your role in the community, your home itself all need to be considered here. Finally, think about what you want to do to develop yourself towards self-fulfilment – courses, reading, travel, hobbies and so on.

Personal Objectives		
	Short-term	Long-term
At work		
At home		
Personal development		

You will undoubtedly have noticed something which you knew all along; achieving those objectives will take two scarce commodities – time and effort. 'If only' you could find both, it would be easy to achieve all of them.

The purpose of this book is to help you to do just that: to improve your personal productivity so that you can find both the time and the effort to translate those objectives into accomplished facts.

Let's get on with it.

Chapter 2
What is Personal Productivity?

Before we start to define personal productivity it will help to decide what 'productivity' itself means because there are a great many confusing ideas as to its real meaning. If you already know what it means, and are used to using it in a production context, you can skip the next few pages and rejoin us when we start to talk about personal productivity.

Productivity

Productivity is a measurement. It measures the relationship between what is produced and the resources involved in the process. Its principal value is that it enables us to compare two or more performances with each other or with a predetermined standard.

For example, let's suppose that two men are making wooden boxes. Albert (A) makes 10 boxes working for 8 hours and Bernard (B) makes 13 boxes working for 9 hours. Assuming the boxes are all equally well made and are identical in all respects, which man is doing the better job – which is the more productive?

A produces 10 boxes for 8 manhours (1 man × 8 hours) of labour input. Therefore the productivity of his labour resource is $^{10}/_8$ which equals 1.25 boxes output per manhour of input.

B produces 13 boxes for 9 manhours of labour input. Therefore the productivity of his labour resource is $^{13}/_9$ which equals 1.4 boxes of output per manhour of input.

So, as far as the use of his time (or manhour resource) is concerned, although he works longer Bernard produces more boxes per manhour than Albert. In fact, we can say that his productivity is 12 per cent higher than Albert's.

$$\frac{1.4 \times 100}{1.25} = 112\%$$

So we give Bernard a rise and Albert a warning. Or do we? First, maybe we ought to look at some of the other resources they both use – for example machinery, or in this case a power-saw.

> A produces 10 boxes using a power-saw for 2 hours, so the productivity of his machine resource is $^{10}\!/_2$ which equals 5 boxes of output per machine hour of input.
>
> B produces 13 boxes using a power-saw for 3 hours, so the productivity of his machine resource is $^{13}\!/_3$ which equals 4.33 boxes of output per machine hour of input.

Here we can see that, when it comes to the use of his machinery resources, Albert is much more productive than Bernard. In fact Bernard's productivity is 13 per cent lower than Albert's:

$$\frac{4.33 \times 100}{5} = 87\%$$

Maybe we had better get Albert to teach Bernard to use the saw more efficiently and that would also help to reduce the amount of time he now uses. But before we make any move perhaps we should look at how the two men compare in their use of the other resource they both use – the material resources or, in this case, the wood they use to make the boxes.

> A produces 10 boxes using 200 metres of planking, so the productivity of his material resource is $^{10}\!/_{200}$ which equals 0.05 boxes of output per metre of wood.
>
> B produces 13 boxes using 210 metres of planking, so the productivity of his material resource is $^{13}\!/_{210}$ which equals 0.06 boxes of output per metre of wood.

How to Get More Done

So, in the use of his material resource too, Bernard is again more productive than Albert, his productivity being a clear 20 per cent higher in fact.

$$\frac{0.06 \times 100}{0.05} = 120\%$$

It looks as if the extra time that Bernard takes over his sawing helps him to save on material, perhaps by cutting more carefully and wasting less. Whether in the final analysis this is more productive or not will depend on checking how they both use the most important resource, which we haven't yet mentioned, and that is – money.

To measure their productivity of the money resource all we have to do is to reduce all the other resource inputs to money to give us a total money input.

A produces 10 units using:

8 manhours' labour at £4	=	32	
2 machine hours at £3	=	6	= 138
200 metres of wood at £0.5	=	100	

Therefore the productivity of his money resource is $10/138$ – equal to 0.072 boxes' output per £1 of input.

B produces 13 units using:

9 manhours' labour at £4	=	36	
3 machine hours at £3	=	9	= 150
210 metres of wood at £0.5	=	105	

Therefore the productivity of his money resource is $13/150$ – equal to 0.087 per £1 of input.

The final result shows that overall, Bernard is more productive than Albert. In fact the combined productivity of all his resources expressed in money terms is 21 per cent better than Albert's.

$$\frac{0.087 \times 100}{0.072} = 121\%$$

So the extra time Bernard takes at the saw bench is more than justified by his more effective use of the costly wood. This is what personal productivity is all about – the more effective use of the resources we have.

Factors affecting productivity

It's interesting to note that, although they were both making the same article, Bernard uses less time and less wood per unit produced than Albert. The effective use of resources, or *utilisation* as it is known in productivity terms, is one of the principal factors affecting productivity.

Resources can be wasted or misused in a variety of ways. Starting late, finishing early or simply being idle for any number of reasons, will decrease the utilisation of time – the manpower resource. Similarly, wasting material by loss, theft, damage or misapplication will decrease its utilisation. As we have seen, reduced utilisation leads to reduced productivity.

The other factor which can affect productivity is *efficiency*, that is the speed and accuracy with which the process is carried out. It was Bernard's efficiency which enabled him to produce more boxes per manhour and per metre of wood. Because of it he made better use of his time and wasted less material which resulted in his over-all productivity being so much higher than that of his workmate.

Of course, there are many other factors which can affect utilisation and efficiency in business such as poor supervision, bad working conditions, lack of motivation, poorly designed processes and so on. Measuring productivity won't improve these but it will often point out where corrective action is necessary to improve productivity. And 'productivity' is the name of the game if you want to succeed in business today.

The previous examples quite obviously refer to the productivity of a business process, converting resources – money, manpower, materials and machinery (the 4Ms) – into products. But where do we come in? What is 'personal productivity'?

Personal productivity

Closely following the above explanation of productivity as it is used in an industrial sense, we can say that personal productivity is a measure of what we get out of our lives compared with what we put in. It's the relationship between the output we obtain and the input of our personal resources. Our only problem is that we won't be able to measure our productivity accurately unless we can clearly identify the output and input in measurable terms. Our difficulties are increased by the fact that many of our outputs don't lend themselves to measurement.

Nor for that matter do many of our inputs, as we shall see later.

The output of a factory or process can be measured in units and the number of units to be achieved can be predetermined and set as an objective. So can the amount of resources required to produce them, which makes the job of measuring productivity in that sort of process relatively easy. We too can set ourselves objectives. Indeed, we have just done so in the last chapter. Some will be easily defined, particularly the tangible objectives connected with our business lives, and progress towards them can be measured.

The more precisely you have stated your objectives the easier it will be for you to measure your progress towards them. As we have said, objectives should describe the result you want to achieve and a time by which you want to achieve it. For example, 'to qualify as a fellow of the Chartered Institute of Marketing by my 35th birthday' is a much more precise objective than 'to learn more about marketing'. Therefore it is much easier to measure progress against it as you complete the various studies and papers.

However, there is a difference between simply making progress and doing so productively – getting the maximum productivity out of our resources. If we are to measure productivity we need to be able to attach some value to our output.

For example, suppose our objective was 'to obtain all of a particular customer's business by the end of the year'. We could give achieving this result a nominal value of 100 so that we could estimate our progress in units and use this to calculate our personal productivity in this particular area. Let's suppose that, after some time, we gained about a third of the business. We could then estimate this as equal to 33 units out of 100.

Progress units achieved to date	=	33
Manhours devoted to customer to date (say)	=	15
Productivity of manhour resource	=	$33/15$
Units of progress per manhour devoted	=	2.2

We could compare this with later measurements or with our progress towards other objectives to see how well we were using our time. Suppose that after a while we manage to gain another 20 per cent of the business.

Progress units achieved since last review	= 20
Manhours devoted to this achievement	= 6
Productivity of manhour resource	= 20/6
Units of progress per manhour	= 3.3

Provided our estimate of progress was reasonably accurate we could congratulate ourselves for improving our productivity by 50 per cent.

$$\frac{3.3 \times 100}{2.2} = 150$$

On the other hand, if the result showed a decrease in our personal productivity we could take action to step up our efforts and make them more effective.

In theory we could use this method to measure progress towards all our other objectives and our personal productivity in the use of our resources. However, because the measurement of progress in many cases would be a rather shaky 'guesstimate', its accuracy would be doubtful and we could probably make more productive use of our time elsewhere. We have only quoted it to demonstrate that, if the need were there, you could measure the productivity of almost any activity.

The important point is not to try for complicated measurements of personal productivity, but to bear the principle constantly in mind so that, whatever you are doing, you are always conscious of the fact that you are committing your resources to the achievement of an objective. The more effectively you use them, the higher your personal productivity will be and the more easily you will achieve your objective.

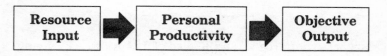

Thinking about productivity in this way shouldn't be confined to the easily defined business objectives. It is particularly valuable to think 'productivity' when working towards the many objectives you will have at home and your personal, perhaps less clearly defined, objectives.

Resources

We have spoken at length of using your resources productively but what, in fact, are your 'resources'? Those you control in your business life are clear – the 4Ms we saw in action earlier. But what about those you use in your personal life? They are obviously very different from those used in the production process but none the less they can be identified, and indeed have to be, if we are to increase their productivity.

The one resource we all have in common is *time*. There are 24 hours in a day, no more, no less, so we all suffer from the same time constraint. The hours of daylight and darkness change with the seasons and to some extent this also acts as a constraint on what we can do – at the moment there aren't too many floodlit golf courses! However, the way we allocate the available time to the things we have to do in order to achieve our objectives is personal to us and here, as we shall see later, is one area where we can vastly improve personal productivity.

Our next major resource is our *personal attributes* – our acquired skills and knowledge, our experience, health, appearance and motivation – all the things that go to make up the unique mix that is us. It has taken many years for us to reach the point we are at today and we need to be sure we are maximising our use of this vital resource.

Another major resource is our *assets* – the material possessions we have acquired such as a house, car, computer, TV etc. It may came as quite a shock to think of these as resources but, depending on your objectives, they may have a large part to play and their productivity can become vital.

The final resource is our *associations* – the family, friends and associates who will give us help, support and comfort when we need it to achieve our objectives.

Mary was shattered when Bill died of a heart attack leaving her to face the future alone for a second time.

They had met and married late in life, both having lost their previous partners through long, drawn out illnesses. In spite of a big gap in their ages, they were well matched and for many years lived a life of great happiness, sharing many interests including music. Mary had been taught music as a girl and still played the cello. All his life Bill wanted to play an instrument but had never had the time to learn. When he retired he used an annuity to buy himself an electronic organ and spent much time (of which he now had an abundance) teaching himself to play. This magnificent instrument intrigued Mary who rapidly became a skilled player and even started to compose short pieces for their joint amusement.

After Bill's death time hung heavily on Mary at first. Then she consoled herself with her music, spending long hours playing the tunes they had enjoyed together.

One day an old friend asked her if she had written any more tunes and this started her thinking it would be a good way to fill her long hours alone. She heard of an amateur song writing contest being held in a neighbouring town and plucked up the courage to enter two of her compositions. On the night of the contest, one reached the finals played by a local pop group. After the contest, the leader, Harry, approached Mary and offered to introduce her to the producer who handled his group.

The producer was impressed with her talent but suggested she work with Harry to improve the arrangements. This she did and the piece was published and did well.

Now she has moved the organ into the spare room which she has converted into a studio and spends a large part of each day composing and working on arrangements with Harry. Last month one of her songs hit the Top 10. When she got back home after the celebration she said a quiet 'Thank you' to Bill whose determination to achieve a life-long objective had indirectly given her the chance to make use of her latent talents.

In that incident Mary used all her resources – time, personal attributes, assets and associations – to achieve a personal objective and to fill a gap in her life. The resources were there largely unused until she set herself an objective and started to make progress towards it. In her case the objective grew as she became more productive; the goal-posts moved back from merely composing a tune to having one broadcast in the Top 10.

This is fairly common. As we reach the top of one mountain we see another over the ridge and redouble our efforts to climb it as well. Increasing your personal productivity will give you the capacity to do this as well.

Perhaps this would be a good time to have another look at those objectives you roughed out in Chapter 1.

Points to remember

1. Productivity is a measure of the relationship between output and input.
2. The resources used in a commercial process are known as the 4Ms – money, manpower, material and machinery.
3. The factors which affect productivity fall under two headings – utilisation and efficiency.
4. Personal productivity is a measure of the relationship between our progress towards an objective and the resources we employ to get there.
5. If they are to be of any use as a measure our objectives must be precisely stated as a result to be achieved in a given time.
6. Our personal resources may be defined as time, personal attributes, assets and associations, all of which have a part to play in the achievement of our objectives.
7. Although it may be difficult to measure outputs and inputs precisely it is important to be conscious of them.
8. Improving personal productivity will always enable you to reach your objectives more quickly and easily.

Chapter 3
Making the Most of Your Time

'It's a waste of time.' How often have you heard that said in the last week or so? Quite often, I would guess, especially if you lead the sort of normal, unco-ordinated life which most of us do. Using the term 'wasted' implies that the time could have been used to better purpose – perhaps more productively.

Time 'management'

Time, as we have established, is one of our resources and it is the way we make use of our resources that affects our personal productivity. You will often hear about 'time management' these days. There are several books on the subject. Many companies send their managers on time management courses. A whole new industry is based on time management, selling portable files which you carry around ostentatiously to show your colleagues and others that you have joined the ranks of the time managers.

The only problem is, of course, that 'time' cannot be managed.

Time exists as a series of measurements recording the duration of the earth's rotation on its own axis and its seasonal changes as it circles around the sun. Its progress is immutable. It cannot be speeded up, slowed down or stopped, however much popular authors would have us believe. 'Time waits for no man' they say ('no person' would be more accurate). Therefore it cannot be managed. The only thing that can be 'managed' is our use of time.

← Discretionary →		← Committed →	
personal	idle	wasted	productive

◄──────── Time Available ────────►

The time available in any period – a day, a week, a month – can be broken down according to how we use it. *Discretionary time* is the time during which we exercise our own discretion over what we do, such as our so-called 'free time' – the time during which we are not committed to any particular activity. Conversely, *committed time* is the time for the duration of which we are committed, voluntarily or by order, to specific activities.

Discretionary time can be split into two – personal time and idle time. Personal time is time we need to take care of our personal survival needs – sleeping, eating, personal hygiene etc. Idle time is time not specifically allocated to any purposeful activity – when we simply allow time to elapse unproductively between one committed activity and the next.

Similarly, committed time can also be split into two – wasted time and productive time. Productive time is spent in actually achieving some purpose to which we are committed in our private or business life. Wasted time is committed time which elapses without any contribution to the purpose to which we are committed. It is wasted in the same way that petrol is wasted if you leave your car engine running while waiting for your partner to visit a shop.

Discretionary ⟶ ⟵ Committed ⟶

sleep	personal hygiene	eating	watching TV	travel	wait	sell
Personal			Idle	Wasted		Productive

If we analysed a day in the life of a sales representative it might look like the diagram above. We have shown productive time (ie face to face with the customer) as being somewhat less than half of the total committed time and less than one eighth of the total time available. This is not artistic licence but a fair approximation of how it works out in practice. And since this face-to-face contact is what the employers pay for you can appreciate their interest in time utilisation.

From the diagram it is obvious that the more of our discretionary time we can commit to productive activities, and the less committed time we waste, the more productive our use of time will be and the higher our personal productivity. The trick is how to increase commitment and how to reduce waste, but before we can start we need to be able to identify both our commitment and the time-wasters.

———— ◊ ————

'I don't know where my day goes.' You've often heard it said, and probably nodded sympathetically. But do you know where yours goes?

Here is a circle representing 24 hours. Make up a pie chart of your own time utilisation by dividing it up into discretionary time (broken down into sleep, personal hygiene, and eating) and committed time (productive time only).

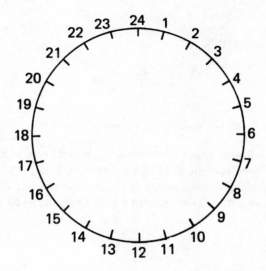

What you have left over is either idle or wasted time. Don't worry if you end up with at least a couple of hours a day in this segment – it's quite normal. Of course, if you drew a pie chart of a weekend day it would probably show a different picture. So to get a true picture of how you spend your time you should really draw a chart covering a week, ie 168 hours.

Simply add up all the time you spend on each activity during a week and mark it off accordingly. For example, you probably spend about 50–60 hours sleeping and so on for the other activities.

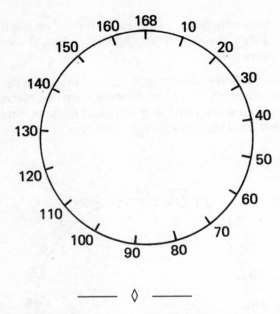

So now you do know where all your time goes and no doubt you are concerned to see how much is idle or wasted. Later we'll look at some ways to reduce this waste but in the meantime it will help if we can identify some of the factors which cause us to be idle or to waste time.

Idle time

Our grandparents used to say that 'the Devil finds work for idle hands', meaning that young people without purposeful activities tend to get up to mischief. Things haven't changed much since their day, although the scale of mischief has escalated. So it would seem that there is considerable moral pressure to avoid or minimise idle time.

We have defined idle time as uncommitted discretionary time. It is spare time available for commitment to activities leading to one or other of our objectives. Time spent in planned leisure or relaxation is not considered as idle time provided the activities are directed towards an objective, such as developing and supporting family relationships by talking and engaging in recreation together. Such time expenditure is considered as 'committed'.

Idle time arises when your objectives are insufficiently

demanding to take up all of the discretionary time you have to spare. For example, if your work and personal objectives demand attention for 12 hours a day and your personal time needs another 10 hours you are left with two hours of idle time to while away in profitless pursuits contributing nothing to your personal objectives. So if you want to increase your personal productivity you will need to keep your idle time to a minimum – assuming you can't eliminate it altogether – and we'll talk about some ways of doing this in the next chapter. Meanwhile let's look at another source of unproductive time.

Wasted time

We have defined wasted time as that portion of the time we have committed to purposeful activities during which progress towards them is stopped for any reason. There are six basic 'progress-stoppers'.

> **Progress-stoppers**
> - Non-objectives
> - No-plans
> - Disorganisation
> - Miscommunication
> - Hi-intrusion
> - Misapplication

Non-objectives

To be effective an objective must be a quantified and timed statement of a measurable result which is reasonably achievable. If you were to say 'I would like to be an accountant', that is a vague expression of an ambition – it is a non-objective. On the other hand, if you were to say, 'I intend to start studying for my accountancy qualifications in May next and to pass all subjects in the qualifying exam in June two years later', you have set yourself an objective which is quantified, timed and measurable. Its very precision will help to motivate you to commence and complete your studies.

Non-objectives enable you to engage in all sorts of activities which are not really helping you to achieve your real aims and therefore, in the final analysis, contribute to wasting your time.

29

—— ◊ ——

'If only', said the old man, 'If only I hadn't wasted so much time as a young man, I could have been rich today. I wanted to be an engineer but I never took the trouble to find out about the courses I had to take. I never set myself an objective and worked towards it. I was too easily diverted to other, more pleasurable pastimes. Life just rolled along.

By the time I reached 40 I felt I was too old, and had too many other commitments to my family to start worrying about a new career. So I let it slide – like I have done with so many things. Anyway, let's not get too serious – have another drink.'

—— ◊ ——

Non-objectives enable us to move the goal-posts. If we can't start it this week, we can do it next week and so on. If our aim is sufficiently important for us to turn it into an objective then we should take the trouble to define it properly and correctly because on our objective depends our plan to get there by a certain time.

Without an objective it is not possible to plan any activity or to set any priorities. Thus, it becomes equally difficult to allocate your available time to important activities. So you allocate time indiscriminately to important and unimportant activities, choosing on the basis of pleasure and ease of completion rather than importance. Fairly soon you've used up all the time you should have been spending on achieving important objectives and, like the old man in the story, you end up missing out on life.

No-plans
To turn an objective into an achievement you need a plan. A plan in its simplest form is a list of the activities that will take you from where you are now to where you want to be in the future. It should proceed logically from step to step until it reaches the objective and it must be timed so that progress from beginning to end can be measured and completion forecast.

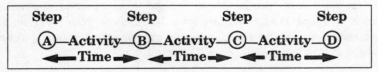

If you don't have a plan, or if your plan doesn't follow a logical sequence (first things first, second things second, last things last), you will waste time and miss opportunities to complete it. If it is not timed you will never know whether you are up to date or behind, and it will stretch indefinitely into the future – a no-plan.

Procrastination is the thief of time, someone once wrote. Well, it's certainly one of them if not the most infamous. Procrastination means simply putting off to tomorrow what you should do today. (Its supporters say, 'Never do today what you can leave until tomorrow.') It means ignoring high priority jobs and concentrating on low priority ones instead.

Procrastination is caused chiefly by our unwillingness to initiate action which may be unpleasant, unaccustomed or difficult, choosing instead to continue with the habitual, the routine, the comfortable. It is aided by a lack of commitment to objectives and the determination to achieve them.

Procrastination is a disease which affects whole nations – the *mañana* syndrome of the so-called Banana Republics – or smaller communities in otherwise energetic countries where it seems to be gaining ground today. The easy way out, the increasing dependency on welfare, acceptance of any excuse to avoid confronting the harsh business of living, these and other signs are common today.

Procrastination means that plans are not laid, or if laid, are not adhered to, so that time is wasted. The 15 minutes spent making up your mind to start a new job is gone for ever. 'Time waits for no one,' as we have said. It runs on unchecked whether we use it or not. You can borrow time from some other activity but you cannot 'make up for lost time'. When it's lost, it's gone for ever.

Procrastination lives on no-plans. If you are not committed to a firm, workable plan you will become a victim of the no-plan virus and fritter away many golden minutes of invaluable time.

Disorganisation

Making a plan happen requires an organisation. That means that the necessary resources – money, people and things – have to be gathered together and arranged so that the right resources are in the right place at the right time to enable the planned activity to take place. If any of the resources are missing disorganisation results and the plan will be held up until they are provided.

Disorganisation is one of the commonest causes of lost time in business and in personal activities.

job. 'Fighting a desk' they call it and it's also a disease. One which causes nervous breakdowns, heart attacks, and premature balding due to the loss of hair pulled out in frustration.

Miscommunication

We often use the term 'misunderstanding' to describe a situation where communication has either arrived distorted or has failed to arrive altogether, so it seems logical that we should refer to the cause of misunderstanding as 'miscommunication'.

Communication is the skill of exchanging information and understanding with another person. Complete communication results in the image in the mind of the receiver being identical to that which started out in the mind of the sender. In order to achieve complete communication the originator or sender passes information to the receiver who confirms understanding by responding in accordance with the sender's objective either by replying or by taking some required action.

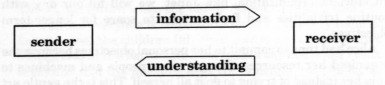

Looks easy, doesn't it? Unfortunately, when people communicate they tend to overlook one important thing.

The area between the sender and the receiver is a minefield, full of all sorts of devices to prevent complete communication and only a brave and skilful communicator can cross it in each direction without suffering severe damage (distortion) to their message. The result is miscommunication.

Telephone rings. Receiver says, 'Hallo.'
Sender, with heavy foreign accent, says, 'Is that Jean?' (Jon) followed by loud crackling noise.
Receiver says, 'Hallo.'
Sender, louder, 'Can you hear me?'
Receiver says, 'There's a lot of noise. Who are you?'
Sender says, 'I'm John. I'm phoning from my car. Is that Jean?'
Receiver says, 'This is (crackle) here, who do you want?'

Sender, getting cross, 'I told you – I want Jean.'
Receiver says, 'But you said *you* were John.'
Sender, really mad now, says, 'I'm John and I want (crackle).
What's the matter with you – don't you speak English?'
Receiver, hanging up, 'Not when you speak it, chum.'

Some of the more common causes of miscommunication are:

Sender
• Lacks clear objective for message
• Fails to assess capability of receiver to understand
• Constructs message badly
• Uses the wrong medium
• Speaks or writes indistinctly
• Chooses an inappropriate time to communicate
• Does not allow for interference or distractions
• Fails to gain full attention

Receiver
• Does not eliminate other distractions
• Does not give message full attention
• Does not listen or read accurately
• Misinterprets message – prejudges its objective
• Fails to check understanding with sender
• Takes action before verifying his/her version

Every time a communication is partially or totally misunderstood time is wasted in corrective action which would not otherwise be necessary. Often the amount of time wasted is considerably greater than that necessary to respond to the communication correctly.

We are talking only of wasted time but the waste of other resources due to miscommunication is often considerably greater in terms of cost, as, for example, when an incorrect action is set in motion.

No better example of the time wasted by miscommunication exists than the average meeting – official or unofficial, business or non-business, planned or impromptu. Meetings take place either to gather information from a group, as in report-back or problem-solving meetings, or to impart information to a group as when briefing participants in a new activity.

A properly organised, prepared and controlled meeting is probably one of the very best means of communication available and in the next chapter we will look at ways of ensuring that they are all productive.

However, for every 'good' meeting you attend you will have to sit through the excruciating boredom and time loss of at least six others. What is the problem? Why do meetings so often result in an unproductive loss of time?

Mismanaged meetings

1. Ad hoc, unplanned, insufficient notice
2. Participants unprepared
3. Participants unable to contribute
4. Chairperson unprepared
5. Insufficient or too much time allowed
6. Interruptions – tea, telephone, other
7. No records kept
8. No decision reached

This table lists only some of the most common reasons – there are many others.

Next time you feel like picking up the phone and telling Jim, Ann and Harry – 'Come up to my office right away. Something's come up' – just think about the work they are doing which will now be disrupted. Think about the meagre input they will be able to make without, at least, making some study of the subject you want to discuss. Think, too, about how you are going to contribute to the success of the meeting without some research of your own.

Think about the lunch appointment you have to keep in 20 minutes and how you are going to fit a productive meeting in before then. And think about the phone call from Tom in the States you are expecting to come through any time now and how much of the others' time will be wasted listening to you and Tom exchanging pleasantries.

Calling ad hoc meetings may be good for the ego but it's awfully bad for productivity.

Hi-intrusion

Time was when managers were taught to adopt the 'ever-open-door' policy. You were not considered to be top management material unless you made yourself available to your staff at any time they felt like talking to you. Managers used to boast about how much of their time was spent in face-to-face contact with their staff.

Today, many years and several thousand stress-induced heart attacks later, we have come to realise that such intrusion into our personal, committed time is not only a terrible waste of our precious time resource but, even more serious, it is an indictment of the way we manage our employees.

Certainly there are times when it is vital that an employee reports directly to you, or asks for help in carrying out an assignment, but they should be exceptions, not the rule.

Harry always took home a briefcase full of work every evening and, after dinner, would shut himself up in his study to go through it, usually finishing long after his wife, Sue, went to bed. When she tackled him about it, which she often did, he would tell her of all the people who had to come to him with problems during the day, and how they depended on him for help. He couldn't let them down, could he? She thought he could and said so. They drifted further apart until they were only a whisker away from divorce.

He took his troubles to his boss, Andrew, asking for an assistant to help him ease the load so he could spend more time with Sue. Andrew knew Sue and admired her for putting up with the situation for so long. 'How can I convince the board that you need help?' he asked Harry.

'Can't you take my word for it?' appealed Harry. 'I can,' said Andrew, 'but they won't unfortunately. Tell you what. Why not keep a log for a week? That will show us both where your time goes.'

'I won't have time to keep it,' replied Harry quickly, anxious to avoid still more work. 'All right,' suggested Andrew, 'why not get Pamela to keep it for you? All she has to do is write down what you are doing every five minutes throughout the day. If she doesn't know she can ask you.'

Harry reluctantly agreed to let his secretary keep a log of his time, and Pamela started the following week. After a week she analysed what she had got and presented it to Harry. It looked like this:

	%
Meetings – own staff	33
Meetings – management	22
Meetings – customers and suppliers	5
Telephone – external calls	10
– internal calls	15
Dealing with mail – external	4
– internal	3
Plans, budgets, projects	8
Working at home	20
	120

Harry was shocked. He was spending 55 per cent of his official working day in ad hoc meetings or interruptions and another 15 per cent on internal calls – a total of 70 per cent in activities which couldn't all be necessary or productive. Meanwhile his vital dealings with customers and suppliers, and the equally important management work of planning was getting only 13 per cent of his time plus whatever he could spare while working at home. If he could halve the time he spent at meetings and talking to subordinates and colleagues he could double this figure and stop taking work home.

He would have to find time to do something about it. Meanwhile, Pamela wanted to see him about the new work routine he'd instituted. He'd better see her first.

Harry's problem is all too common and we'll discuss ways of solving it in the next chapter. Meanwhile let's look at the last of the progress-stoppers.

Misapplication
One of the principal causes of low productivity in business is poor quality work resulting in rejects. When the product does not meet laid down standards, it has to be scrapped and all the time, effort

and materials used in producing it are lost.

The need to minimise this misapplication of resources is becoming recognised and many businesses are adopting the Japanese concept of perfect quality or 'right first time', aimed at eliminating rejects altogether.

There are many reasons for misapplication, which can include poor planning, poor design, poor quality materials and, perhaps most common of all, lack of knowledge or skill. If we do something wrongly then we have to do it again and that's a waste of time apart from anything else.

Misapplication doesn't only affect production situations, it can reduce our personal productivity in almost any activity from running a business to running a household and lead us to waste huge amounts of time while we repeat activities which we should have got right the first time.

With so many progress-stoppers working against us it's a wonder we manage to achieve any of our objectives at all. Yet we do. But how much more could we achieve if we could eliminate at least some of them, as we shall see in the next chapter?

Points to remember

1. Time cannot be managed but its utilisation can.
2. Time available can be broken down into discretionary time, which includes personal and idle time, and committed time, which includes wasted and productive time.
3. Idle time is defined as uncommitted discretionary time. Wasted time is defined as that portion of committed time when progress towards an objective is halted for any reason.
4. Managing your utilisation of time means concentrating on idle time and wasted time to endeavour to minimise them.
5. The six factors which halt progress, or 'progress-stoppers' as we call them, are:

   Non-objectives
   No-plans
   Disorganisation
   Miscommunication
   Hi-intrusion
   Misapplication.

Chapter 4
Planning Your Strategy

We saw earlier that before we can make any attempt to improve productivity we have first to measure how we are doing now so that we can see exactly where improvement is needed. You did this in the last chapter by filling in a pie chart showing your guesstimate of how you spent the 168 hours available in a week.

If you want to do this accurately you will have to keep a simple time log of your activities (like the one Pamela kept for Harry in the story in the last chapter) which is a record of what you are doing every five minutes of the day.

Time Log							Date									
Hrs	07	08	09	10	11	12	13	14	15	16	17	18	19	20	21	22
Mins 05	)	)	E	F	F	E	B	D	F	F	C	A	A	B	A	
10	(	(	D			E		D	|	|	|	|	|	|		
15	A	C	D			D		E	|	|	|	|	|	|		
20	(	(	E			D		D	|	|	|	|	|	|		
25	)	)	D			E		E	|	|	|	|	|	|		
30	)	)	D			E		D	|	|	|	|	|	|		
60	B	D		|	|		F		D							

Summary
A = 90 B = 90 C = 90 D = 75 E = 40 F = 240

A = Personal   D = Desk Work
B = Meals   E = Telephone
C = Travel   F = Meetings (internal)

In order to fill in the log you need first to make up a simple code to cover your activities. For example, A = Personal time, B = Meals, C = Travel, and so on. If you want to make it really useful you can break work time down into the various things you do at work, such as meetings, phoning etc.

As you go through the day you enter a code letter against the time, as has been done in the example. At the end of the day, when you have a spare moment, you can add them up. Adding the totals at the end of the week will tell you exactly how you have used your time and you can compare this with the estimate you made in the last chapter. You may get a shock, particularly if you have been honest!

If you want a guide as to how your utilisation of time compares with the way others use it, here are some generally accepted average figures.

Personal time	77	
Travel/commute	10	
Work	45	— Total 168 hours per week
Family/leisure	30	
Idle	6	

If you think that recording every five minutes is too often in your case then make up the form to record every 15 minutes using the same code. However you decide to do it, the time log is a vital starting point in your search for improved productivity.

Where to start

We have decided how we presently use our available time; now we have to decide whether we are using it productively or not. This means we have to go back to our objectives and decide whether the progress we are making towards them is enough or whether we ought to try to improve it. In the latter case we will need to allocate more resources to achieving that particular objective without jeopardising the achievement of all our other objectives. Where are these extra resources going to come from?

We are only looking at the time resource at present and, working from the log you have completed, the obvious place to start is idle time (assuming you have been honest and recorded some). Idle time, as we saw in Chapter 3, is time which we have not specifically allocated to a purposeful activity and its presence indicates the effect of one or other of the first two progress-stoppers – *non-objectives* or *no-plans*.

Non-objectives will cause idle time to occur because they encourage a lack of commitment and urgency in their achievement.

'I know I really should fix the light in the hall but it's so pleasant sitting here looking at the garden and enjoying the sun.'

'We had intended to go away to the country this week but it's such a business packing up the house and fixing up accommodation and everything. So we just stayed at home and did nothing.'

'The chairman didn't tell us why he had called the meeting so we just sat there and waffled for 10 minutes until he finally did. What a waste of time – there were 15 people there!'

Setting clear objectives

In the last chapter we agreed that, to be effective, an objective must be:

> - Precise
> - Quantified
> - Timed
> - Accepted
> - Achievable

Unless an objective is *precisely stated* it is worse than useless. A fire chief saying to his men, 'Go and put the fires out!' may sound good on TV but it is unlikely to achieve the same result as giving them a precise location. Similarly, 'I want to be a sales manager some day' is somewhat less effective as a motivator than 'I want to obtain the IOM qualification for sales management this year and then apply to World Wide Corporation for an area manager's job.'

Only if the objective is *quantified* will we be able to judge our progress towards it. 'To increase production' is a worthwhile aim, but unless we know by how much we will never know if our progress is good or bad, whereas, 'To increase production from 100 to 150 per day' enables us to measure our progress as our production slowly improves.

However, even that objective doesn't say 'when' we have to reach the new target so we are in danger of contracting the mañana syndrome. If we add a *time-limit* to that objective – 'by 30th December' – we will know precisely how we are doing at any time and what effort we need to apply to reach it on time.

If an objective is to have the power to motivate us towards its achievement we must *wholeheartedly accept it* as worthwhile otherwise it will not be strong enough to compete with all the other desires and distractions to which we are subjected. This is particularly the case when work objectives are handed down to us from above. If we don't fully understand and accept them we will probably not be inclined to put in that little extra effort needed to clinch them.

An American university carried out a survey on six similar building sites to study the effect of participation in setting objectives on results achieved. First, they devised a series of measurements to enable them to monitor the output of each site over the six-month-long test.

Then they arranged for the objectives to be set in conjunction with the managers on three of the sites and to be imposed from the head office on the remainder. The feedback of results for each site was also varied, ranging from the sites measuring their own, through critical feedback, to having no feedback at all.

At the end of the test, the researchers found that the output from the site which was participating in setting its own objectives and developing its own feedback of results exceeded that of the site which had no objectives and no feedback by no less than 30 per cent, the others falling somewhere in between.

This finding supports the view that the acceptance of an objective by the person concerned is vital if he or she is to have a reasonable chance of achieving it.

Finally, we must recognise the objective as being *achievable*. If it is difficult to achieve, that's good because it will stimulate us to greater effort. But if it is really beyond our capacity we will soon lose heart and interest in the operation, achieving even less than our normal output.

A good practical way to set up objectives which will meet all five points is to take the time to write them down in a statement which should set out precisely:

What has to be achieved	(A desired result)
Why it has to be achieved	(Justification)
When it has to be achieved	(Time-limits)
Who will achieve it	(People involved)
Where it must be done	(Place involved)

'Now is the time for all good men to come to the aid of the Party' would be more effective as an objective if written as 'All males over 21 of impeccable character, each vouched for by two independent witnesses, must apply to join the Party within the next two days.'

As you see, this certainly takes a bit longer but at least progress towards our objectives (or the lack of it) can be measured and action taken to jack up performance if necessary.

Planning made easy

'No-plans' also contribute to idle time because if they are badly timed or, worse, are not timed at all we will either put off starting them or else finish them early and find we have time 'on our hands'.

People will often tell you that 'Planning is a waste of time because you always have to change it as you go along anyway.' But the same people would not dream of taking a walk in the country without plotting their route on a map and following it from point to point – in other words, planning their route. Shopping in a supermarket with someone who has no list of the goods required is a boring (and expensive) business as the trolley is slowly over-filled with impulse purchases. In business, unplanned or imperfectly planned events can cost millions.

In order to plan you need three things:

- Time
- Objective
- Method

Planning takes *time* to do properly. If you try to grab a few minutes here and there you will end up with a no-plan. So, before you do anything else, allocate a definite time for planning. In business this means closing your 'ever open door', unplugging the phone, and getting down to it. At home, it means waiting until other members of the family are safely out of the way before settling down with paper and pencil (and an eraser!).

The next basic need is a clearly defined *objective* (preferably in writing) which should state an achievable result – ie 'to complete Course A at the Language School by September' *not* 'to learn French this year'. 'To improve the ratio of prospecting calls to customer calls to 1 in 5 by September' *not* 'Improve prospecting.'

Next you have to decide on the *method*, ie the critical results (CRs) you will have to achieve on the way to your objective.

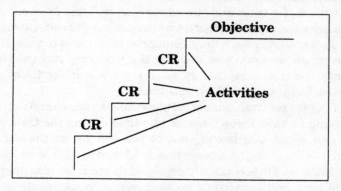

It's rather like walking up stairs. The landing is your objective but to reach it you have first to climb each step on the way. Reaching each step is a critical result because if you miss it out you won't reach the landing. Moving from one CR to another takes effort (ie the use of resources) and is known as an 'activity' or 'task'. So, in its simplest form, a plan is a list of the activities necessary to achieve the CRs and finally reach the objective.

1. Draw money from bank
2. Drive to station
3. Catch 11.30 train
4. Arrive 14.30
5. Hire taxi
6. Arrive at mother's 15.15

Suppose you wanted to visit your aged mother in the

country. You could draw up a simple list of activities like that. Or you could show them graphically like this:

Time	10	11	12	13	14	15	16
Get money	▭						
To station		▭					
On train				▭▭▭▭▭			
In taxi							▭

In this plan, drawing the money and driving to the station are of critical importance because if you don't achieve either of them you won't be on the train and the whole plan will fail. In every plan there are some critical activities which you need to concentrate on to ensure nothing goes wrong. Similarly, most plans contain time-spans when someone else is doing the worrying and the work, leaving you free to relax – as when the train driver takes over between 11.30 and 14.30. Or can you?

It's easy to see from this sort of plan (called a bar chart) that you are going to have three hours of idle time during the train ride. You can spend this looking out of the window at the passing countryside or reading a magazine or whatever – all of which are unproductive. Or you can decide ahead to use it for planning the rest of your visit or catching up with your correspondence or any number of productive activities leading to worthwhile objectives.

Time	10	11	12	13	14	15	16
Get money	▭						
To station		▭					
On train				▭▭▭▭▭			
In taxi							▭
Planning				▭▭▭▭▭			

Pre-planning your available time has become big business and there are all sorts of expensive diaries, files, pocket computers and suchlike available. Anything that helps you to plan the more effective use of your time is a help but you can achieve the same result for virtually no cost by using the *Daily Action Plan* (see overleaf).

This form is completed each day and you will have to set aside 10–15 minutes the evening before to filling it in. First, enter the phone calls you have to make in the upper left columns and below that the people you have to see and when. Then fill in the *must do* columns on the right of the page. The *before* column will enable you to set deadlines for completion of each item and the time or date will set the *order* in which you place them. Finally jot down things you want to remember in the space at the bottom of the form.

If you use the form conscientiously you will find your day going more smoothly and a reduction in the pressure of work. That's a worthwhile reward for 10 minutes' work each evening, isn't it?

So, rededication to our personal objectives and overhauling our plans to get there will go a long way towards reducing idle time. But what about all the other time-consuming activities we have uncovered? Is this time expenditure contributing to our objectives?

The only way to find out is to check from the time log how we are using the time at present and then ask ourselves a series of questions about each activity.

---

1. What objective is the activity aimed at?   (*Precision*)
2. Do I still feel the objective is worthwhile?   (*Priority*)
3. Would better planning help me use less time?   (*Planning*)
4. Could I achieve more in the time I now use?   (*Productivity*)
5. Where would I apply the time saved?   (*Preference*)

Applying these questions to the time usage areas you have established will help you to examine each one critically and rededicate your efforts to the objectives you have set yourself.

Personal time

For example, check your personal time. The objective of the time you allocate to sleeping is to allow the body to recover from the drain on its physical and mental resources incurred during the day. The average person can normally achieve this in seven to eight hours of interrupted sleep, say up to 56 hours per week. If you are using more than this it is either because you need it for

Work Plan   Date _____   Day _____

| MUST PHONE | | | | MUST DO | | | MUST REMEMBER |
when	number	who	why	order	what	before	

| MUST MEET | | | |
when	where	who	why

some medical reason or, and more probable, because your other objectives are not sufficiently demanding and you are lolling about in bed instead of getting up and facing the world. In either case the answer is in your hands (or your doctor's).

A similar examination of the other components of personal time may lead you to change some priorities and rellocate your time accordingly.

Commuting/Travelling

As the workforce grows and the transport infrastructure deteriorates so we all seem to be spending more and more of our lives simply getting to and from our place of work. At first sight there doesn't seem to be too much you can do about it, but like all the other examples of time utilisation, it may bear closer examination. There are three options:

> 1. Eliminate it altogether
> 2. Reduce it
> 3. Combine it with another activity

The recent tremendous improvement in telecommunications, coupled with such developments as personal computers, modems, fax machines and desk-top publishing, have enabled many professional, clerical and accounting employees to work from home and thus eliminate or substantially reduce their commuting. Indeed, due to the general shortage of skills, many progressive organisations are encouraging this departure from normal practice because it facilitates the use of part-time employees. You might be able to come to an arrangement where you work at home at least one day a week, which would give you a saving of 20 per cent of your commuting time.

The most obvious way to reduce commuting time is to move nearer to your work. This goes against the current trend of the upwardly mobile workers which seems to be to move as far as possible from their place of work. However, there are signs of companies relocating to areas where the quality of life is improved and commuting reduced. So joining one of them is an option, particularly if your objectives tend towards family life rather than work life.

If you can't change your job then try to change your hours of travel – earlier or later. Many companies encourage 'flexitime' wherein employees are free to set their own times as long as they are present for a fixed period of 'core time' when everyone has to be there. This enables their employees to travel at off-peak hours when it's less congested.

Combining another activity with commuting is an option well known to seasoned commuters using public transport who studiously read their papers and work on reports carried in the ubiquitous briefcase. However, overcrowding has affected even these stalwarts, while those who commute by car would find it difficult to concentrate on their accounts in the middle of a traffic jam.

For both of these help is at hand in the shape of the pocket tape recorder which started its career clamped to the ears of young rock fans but has now achieved respectability as a means of constructively using commuting time. Tapes are available covering a multitude of topics which can contribute to personal learning and advancement objectives while radio programmes such as *Open University* or *University of the Air* can be taped to help fill the commuting hours.

The car or portable telephone is another aid to the busy person anxious to make better use of enforced idleness; careful planning of calls while travelling can release valuable work time for more productive activities. Whatever you decide to do, time saved from commuting is a bonus you can add to leisure, family or personal time.

Family and leisure time

Have you noticed, when you and your partner have completed a piece of DIY work together in the house or garden, and you stand back to admire it, what a wonderful sense of satisfaction and pleasure you experience? And how long it lasts?

The experts call this 'achievement satisfaction' and it is one of the strongest forces which motivate people to make an effort. In business we are taught that encouraging people to set their own objectives and then helping them to achieve them is a sure way to increase their productivity, particularly when they can work as a team and share the goals between them.

Why not have another look at the objectives you set yourself in Chapter 1, particularly your personal and family objectives? Do they include your partner or family? How could you include them? Could you set up some new objectives in conjunction with them which you could share and work towards together? If you can do this it will not only improve the productivity of your time but will vastly improve the quality of your joint lives.

When he was promoted to sales manager, John's boss persuaded him to join the local golf club. 'You'll find a lot of the people you meet there will be able to help you and we'll pick up the tab so it won't cost you anything if you don't drink too much.'

John bought a set of clubs, which he could ill afford, found a sponsor and was duly elected a member. He took lessons and practised hard in his 'spare' time. Quite soon he could play to his handicap and took part in the regular Saturday competitions. It wasn't long before he was playing on Wednesdays too, taking work home and using Sunday morning to catch up on what he had missed at the office.

The ritual of the '19th hole' quickly claimed him (after all, he was supposed to meet people) and his family had to get used to seeing him late in the evening on golf nights and usually somewhat the worse for wear.

One day someone ran into the back of his car at a traffic light and he suffered a dislocated neck. When he recovered he started to play golf again but found that somehow his co-ordination had been affected and his game was poor and most frustrating. Eventually, after several months of bad-tempered effort, he gave up the game altogether.

His wife and family received the news with mixed feelings. They had got used to doing things on their own and were not overjoyed at the prospect of long hours in his grumpy company. His wife called a council of war and told him of their feelings. He was shattered at first. He had not realised how his selfish addiction to the game had affected them and began to regret the many hours of discretionary time he had squandered.

The family decided on an objective to spend Saturdays together on domestic chores and to spend Sundays introducing the children to nature study. They bought books on animals and birds and some field-glasses and maps.

John found his old army training a help with the pathfinding, his wife enjoyed catering for the picnic lunches and being out in the open air, while the children became expert at spotting and recognising the wildlife. At the end of each day together they could relax in the warm glow of having achieved a shared objective.

At the beginning of this chapter we asked ourselves the question 'Where shall we start?' and the answer is clearly that we start by measuring how we are using time at present. Once we know this we need to set up clear and meaningful objectives that we want to achieve and then plan to achieve them.

Whether or not you will reach your objectives will depend very much on your determination and application. No amount of planning will take the place of your real dedication to achieve greater personal productivity.

Points to remember

1. The best way to find out how you spend your time now is to make up a time log.
2. The chief causes of idle time are 'non-objectives' and 'no-plans'.
3. To be effective objectives must be precise, quantified, timed, accepted and achievable.
4. In order to plan effectively you need time, a clear objective and a method.
5. A critical result (CR) is an important result on the way to your objective.
6. An activity is the work required to move from one CR to another.

Chapter 5
Getting Help

We've made some progress. We have a clear, quantified and timed objective. We have a practical plan to achieve it. All we need now is to make it work – it's as simple as that. Or is it?

Unfortunately, this is the area where disorganisation rears its ugly head and causes the best laid plans to fail miserably. How can we avoid this common progress-stopper?

The first step is to understand the enemy and agree on what we mean by being 'organised' as opposed to 'disorganised'.

Organising is another word that we use loosely and often out of its correct context. 'Organise me a cup of tea, won't you, Alice.' (Meaning: 'I know it's not your job but I need a cup of tea and you know how to find one for me.') Or, 'I'm relying on you to organise the shareholders' meeting, John.' (Meaning: 'I shall hold you responsible for setting objectives, planning, organising and controlling the shareholders' meeting so that nothing goes wrong.')

Organising

In the context of productivity, organising means simply the work of obtaining, holding and administering the resources we need to carry out a particular plan. The plan (if we have drawn it up properly) describes the events we want to accomplish and the steps we will have to take to reach them. Organising starts by calculating the resources that will be needed to complete each step.

This is probably the most vital part of organising anything – from a picnic to a sea-borne invasion – just working out what will be required, because anything omitted from your calculation will not be available when it is needed and the result will be disorganisation and a consequent loss of productivity.

Efficient hostesses planning a party know this only too well and make lists of all the items they are likely to need. In business it's far safer to make such lists than to rely on memory and luck.

The meeting started 10 minutes late because three of the people concerned hadn't been warned. The air-conditioning in the meeting room wasn't working because the maintenance staff had dismantled it for routine maintenance.

There weren't enough chairs at first and the secretary had to carry in two from an adjoining office. She also had to go to Stationery and get pads and pencils and a pen for the white-board that the manager wanted to use to illustrate his plans for increased productivity. He later discovered that there was no eraser and had to hold up his presentation until one was brought.

As he started his presentation the tea trolley arrived and it took another five minutes before everybody was served. After 15 minutes the MD put his head round the door and said, 'Robert, I suppose you know the Finance Committee is meeting here at half past?'

When the meeting closed 10 minutes later there had been no time to discuss the manager's proposals and the ten people present had each wasted 40 minutes or a total of 6 ½ hours of executive time. If the manager had spent a fraction of that time listing his requirements and ensuring they were available he might have achieved his planned objective and used his manpower resource more productively.

Before you can take the next step to obtain what you will require you need to know what you have already. The hostess has a fairly good idea of where everything is and can check it out quite easily.

Not all business people have equally efficient data banks although today the use of personal 'organisers' or over-blown diaries is common. Developments in this field include data base programmes for personal computers, portable computers and even hand-held microcomputers which can hold as much information as several filing cabinets. Whatever you use, the important thing is to be able to find what you have when you need it.

The only way to ensure this is to develop personal tidiness. 'A place for everything and everything in its place,' so runs the old adage and it's as fundamental today as it was whenever it was first spoken. People who work in confined spaces (sailing yachts, airliner galleys and similar problem areas) quickly learn that if things are not kept in their place you can never find them when you want them – usually in an emergency. So a little time spent in arranging your work environment, whether at home or at work, will pay handsome dividends when you have to find the resources you need to implement a plan.

The 4 Rights

So we now know what we need, what we already have, and the balance which we have to obtain before we can start work on the plan. The key here is the ability to provide the 4 Rights for every plan we make or are presented with.

The key to effective organisation is the provision of

- the *right* amount of
- the *right* resource at
- the *right* place at
- the *right* time to

enable the plan to be executed

Obtaining the right *amount* means there will be no waste or shortage of that particular resource. It is easy to overprovide – just to be on the safe side, as we say. Often we do this deliberately to avoid the trauma of shortages of vital resources caused by our failure to estimate requirements accurately. The result (for the hostess) is a fridge full of left-overs gathering listeria or whatever the latest bug is and for the businessman a stockroom cluttered with unwanted stock tying up much-wanted cash. At the personal level overprovision will result in unproductive resources, particularly idle time, which we want to avoid.

Obtaining the right *resources* is equally vital. Here we must include not only our personal resources of time, personal attributes, possessions and associations, but also those material resources we control in our jobs – the money, manpower, materials and machinery which make up the resources of an organisation.

In business today the buzz word is 'Quality' because we have at last relearned the lesson the Japanese learned from us 40 years ago and have since exploited in the world's markets. The lesson is simply that in the final analysis it is more profitable to produce a 'quality' item than to produce junk, but to do so requires that all the inputs have to be of equal quality too.

Obviously the quality must match the particular need we are planning to fill. Quality means that the product will adequately meet the requirements of the job it has to do and will not fail in service. Providing excess quality beyond this point is obviously a waste of resources and unproductive.

So, when seeking the resources you need to carry out any plan, you should set yourself strict standards of the quality needed to do a 'quality' job and resist accepting inferior substitutes.

Providing the resources at the right *place* would seem to be so elementary as not to need stressing. It's amazing how many people think that once the goods have been ordered they have no further responsibility and it's up to those who want them to ensure delivery. Until the resources are at the spot where they are going to be used they are useless and idle time will mount up until they are delivered.

Finally the resources must be available when needed – at the right *time* – otherwise there will be delay and more idle time will build up. It is a common fault to underestimate the time it will take to assemble the resources to carry out a plan. This is the area where our best intentions can suffer from Murphy's Law – 'If it's possible for things to go wrong, they will!' – and we have to create a fine balance between delivering too early and delivering 'just-in-time'.

Those who are experienced in the 'just-in-time' technique will tell you that the secret lies in your relationship with your suppliers, which has to change from the traditional adversarial attitudes, where each side tries to take advantage of the other, to a position of mutual trust and co-operation. Only then can you expect to achieve the 4 Rights every time.

Delegation

Organising takes time and can easily eat into both your discretionary and committed time unless you can get help. There are two ways you can get help: either allocate some of the jobs to someone else or delegate them. What's the difference? It's small but very important.

When you allocate work to other people you hold them responsible for carrying out a task under your supervision. You plan it and organise it and see that they do it. They can only do what you tell them and may not use their own initiative or change the assignment in any way without reference to you. Allocation is widely used in most organisations, particularly for repetitive work where initiative and latitude are not necessary.

Allocating some of your chores to others will relieve you of the physical labour of doing them and so save you some time for other things, but you will still be left with all the planning and organising to do as well as the task of constantly supervising the person doing the work. The only way to reduce the time thus spent is to delegate.

When you delegate you pass on not only the *responsibility* for getting it done but also the *authority* to do so without reference to you. This enables the person to whom you have delegated the job to get on with it without your constant supervision, simply advising you when it has been done and thus releasing large amounts of your time for more productive work that only you can do.

In every situation there are some things that only you can do because they require special knowledge or skill, or perhaps they have been specifically entrusted to you and are confidential. These cannot be delegated but apart from these there are usually many boring and time-wasting tasks that can. The best way to find them is to make up a review of the work you do at present.

| **Work Review** | | |
Work I do now	**Why I must do it (or)**	**It could be done by**

The work review asks you to list all the work you do now and then to answer one of two questions. Either why it must be done by you or, if there is no special reason, the name of the person to whom you could delegate it. If you haven't done this exercise before, and you fill this form in honestly, you will be amazed at how much of what you do could be done by someone else, leaving you free to spend more of your time on more important matters.

So, having seen the considerable benefits to be gained from delegation, how do we go about it? The easiest way is to follow the routine of *planned delegation*.

Planned Delegation

1. Check delegatee has time and skill.
2. Explain what has to be done in detail and define the limits of authority.
3. Agree the standards by which the work will be evaluated.
4. Agree deadlines and reporting procedure.
5. Monitor the results and give guidance if necessary but

don't take it back

It's not much use trying to delegate something if the person to whom you are delegating has no spare time in which to do it. Sometimes you will find that their lack of spare capacity is because they too are suffering from disorganisation and that will have to be tackled first. The easiest way to do this is to have them complete a time log (see Chapter 4) after which they will usually find they have some underused time.

They may claim they don't have time because they think the job is too complicated or demanding; in this case you not only have to reassure them but also convince them of the benefit to them of expanding their knowledge and experience. Many people do not have to employ their full talents in their jobs and are often glad to have the opportunity to do something more interesting and important – it increases their job satisfaction.

It goes without saying that the delegatee must have the necessary skill to do the job. Here it may be necessary to 'fragment' the job, that is to break it down and to take out any difficult bits that they can't do, keeping these yourself. Most of the things we do are a mixture of simple and difficult tasks, very often the simple ones taking up the bulk of the time.

In her job with a leading stockbroker, Elizabeth had to produce a monthly report on the section of the market that she covered. This was then printed and circulated to all the company's clients. It contained a great number of tables which had to be calculated and set out in a particular format for the printers. Setting it out took a lot of time.

As the deadline approached each month Elizabeth spent more and more time on it, often working late into the night to meet the deadline and always worried that the constant pressure would cause her to make a mistake in a vital calculation.

One day, in the washroom, she met one of the office typists who confided in her that she had just completed a business diploma course at night school and was bored stiff by the routine typing she was stuck with. Elizabeth asked if she would like to help with the monthly reports. The typist was enthusiastic and they spent time together fragmenting the job so that the typist would do all the formatting of the report while Elizabeth concentrated on the all-important numbers and forecasts.

Now Elizabeth has time to spend on all the other important aspects of her job and the monthly report goes out like clockwork. The typist really enjoys using more of her skills and has introduced several new and attractive formats which greatly improve the impact of the reports.

Once you have found someone to delegate a job to, the next, and vital, step is to define clearly the authority you are delegating. If possible this should be sufficient to allow the job to be completed without reference to you although, at first, you may want to limit it until you see how well the job is done. However, it should be your aim to give full authority as soon as possible.

A point to remember is that although you may authorise someone else to do something on your behalf you remain responsible overall that it is done. In other words, 'delegation' doesn't mean 'abdication'.

As part of the delegation process you will have to agree with the person concerned the standards by which both of you will judge whether the work has been correctly done. These should be precise and measurable so that there can be no argument as to whether they have been reached or not. Setting clear standards not only makes your job of monitoring easier but also helps the delegatee to take a pride in the work and gain job satisfaction from doing it well.

The standards should also include the deadlines that have to be met and the type and frequency of reporting you require so that you will not have to make constant nagging enquiries as to how things are progressing which will waste more of your time and upset the delegatee.

Finally, you will need to monitor the reports you receive to see that standards are being met, give guidance if they are not and praise and thanks if they are. Whatever you do, don't ignore the last advice in the box on page 58 and take the job back. If you do you will have wasted all the time you spent on delegating it and returned to your old time-wasting habits. Even more serious, you will have permanently damaged your relationship with the delegatee.

An extension of delegating which can also contribute to a more productive use of time is the *practice of completed staff work* which lays down that when you want to refer a problem to another for a decision you must present both the problem *and* your proposed solution together. This prevents you from offloading your problems or passing the buck and makes decision-making much easier for whoever is faced with it. It also makes buck-passing more difficult and encourages people to solve their own problems without encroaching on your time resource.

It works equally well when you are at the receiving end and training your people to apply it will save you much valuable time. 'Don't bring me problems to solve – bring me solutions to approve' should be displayed in large letters above your workplace.

Management by objective

A method by which delegation and control may be formalised is the procedure known under many titles, the best known of which is management by objective (MBO). This requires that everyone concerned should have a clear work objective and know the results required to achieve it. From this they can determine the steps or activities necessary to get there.

Installing MBO follows much the same steps as we have suggested for planned delegation, the first being the determination of the job objective.

Job Objective – Storeman

To ensure that all materials for the production line are received, stored and issued correctly in accordance with current procedures.

The job objective is a simple statement of the reason why the job was created and exists – in this case to ensure the correct handling and recording of incoming materials.

The next step is for the manager and storeman to work out together the intermediate results that have to be achieved if that objective is going to be met. These critical results have to be measurable so that both parties can see when they are being met. So each will be accompanied with a 'standard' just the same as we used in delegation.

Critical Results	Standards
1. All material accepted into the store meets order specification.	Nil defects in material stored.
2. Storage space is fully used.	Utilisation is
3. Etc.	kept over 95%.

Note that each critical result (CR) is written as a 'result', ie something that has happened and can therefore be measured. Once the critical results have been agreed, the employee can list the activities necessary to achieve each one and the manager can delegate specific authority to enable the employee to work without constant reference to him or her.

CR No	Activities	Authority
1/1	Check each consignment against order specification	Full
1/2	Accept consignments that match	Full
	Reject consignments that don't	Refer to
1/3		Purchasing

If critical results, standards and activities are recorded in a formal job description then control is simply a matter of reviewing performance against standards from time to time and taking corrective action or praising where appropriate.

The key to this review is the action plan, which should be drawn up by the employee and approved by the manager. Action plans are usually drawn up as a result of a formal annual appraisal of session or a periodic review of results, either monthly or quarterly, depending on the degree of delegation operating.

Action Plan			
CR/Activity	Action required	By when	Results
2.0	Improve utilisation from 80% to standard 95%	1.3.91	Reached 85% by 1.10.90

This lists all the critical results which are not being achieved and the action that will be taken to achieve them. The person drawing up the plan commits him/herself to a completion date without which the plan is a no-plan and valueless. The plan can be reviewed as often as the manager feels is necessary and the opportunity used to add or delete items.

Organising your employees' work in this manner will vastly reduce the unnecessary calls on your time stemming from disorganisation. Indeed, if you can set up a similar system for yourself, it will help you to focus on your own critical results and objectives with a correspondingly beneficial effect on your own time utilisation and productivity.

You don't have to be in business to benefit from MBO. You can use it to organise your approach to your personal objectives, breaking them down into critical results, standards and activities in exactly the same way. The only difference is that you will be the employer and will make your own reviews when it suits you. Used in this way it will organise your personal plan and force you to do something about achieving it and moving towards your overall objective, whatever that is.

It will work even better if you can involve the rest of your family in the whole process starting with discussing and agreeing mutual objectives and ending up with shared responsibilities, rather like Alice in Chapter 3. That would be worth a few minutes with pen and paper, wouldn't it?

Points to remember

1. Organising is the work of obtaining, holding and administering the resources needed to carry out a plan.
2. The first step in organising is to calculate the resources needed to achieve the plan's objective.

Gaining attention

Remember we talked about the minefield of other inputs lying between the sender and the receiver which contributes to miscommunication? The only way to get across it safely is to gain the attention of the receiver before you start. There are many ways you can do this – clap your hands, drop something, make a joke, scream. But the most effective way is to refer to the other person's objectives.

He or she may not have spent as much time defining them as we hope you have as a result of your work on this book but, nevertheless, everyone has objectives of sorts. If people can sense that you are either threatening or assisting their achievement they will certainly pay you attention – at least until they find out what you want of them.

'I liked your presentation. It went well.'
'You have an excellent manner with children.'
'I can see you're very ambitious.'
'I have some bad news for you.'
'You are well known for your perception.'

Most of these examples have an element of praise in them because, provided it sounds reasonably genuine, we all enjoy being praised and will tend to listen favourably to anyone who thinks well of us. Threatening a person's security will certainly attract attention but their attitude to what follows may not be so favourable.

This method applies to both spoken and written communication. It is just as important to gain the favourable attention of a reader as of a listener and the same approach works equally well on both.

'Thank you for your very prompt reply.'
'I'm sure you will find . . . '
'Here's something that will appeal to you as . . . '
'Do you ever wonder . . . ?'

Arousing interest

Now that you have the listener's attention you must be quick to consolidate your position by arousing his/her interest in what you have to say. There are many ways of doing this but perhaps the most effective is to continue your initial approach and refer to the listener's objective as you know it, suggesting how it may be affected by what you have to say.

'I liked your presentation. It went well. Have you ever thought how much easier you would find it to explain the complicated part in the middle if you used some well chosen slides?'

You will notice that we have deliberately avoided the trap of criticising the presentation as lacking clarity. Criticism causes us to become defensive and to start thinking of ways to justify our actions. This effectively blocks off our listening and causes miscommunication to take place. So, if you want to arouse interest, keep it positive.

Filling in detail

This is the part of the process where you have to get down to what you want to communicate and clearly state your message in terms of what, when, where and how. At the same time you want to maintain the co-operative attitude you have created and to achieve this you will need to add 'why' to your message.

Tennyson's oft-quoted 'Theirs not to reason why, theirs but to do and die' might have got cavalrymen to charge in the Crimean War but it wouldn't move many tanks today. Today we expect to participate in decisions and gain considerable satisfaction from being party to them. This means that when you want someone to do or consider something you have to tell them the 'why' behind it if at all possible. And, of course, the 'why' should be phrased so as to indicate clearly how they will be affected (preferably favourably) if they respond to your message.

'I liked your presentation. It went well. Have you ever thought how much easier you would find it to explain the complicated part in the middle if you used some well chosen slides?

If you will pick out the areas where you think they will help and do some rough sketches before Monday, I will get them made up professionally and get them back to you in time for your big presentation on Friday. That way there will be less chance of those important clients missing the message by not paying attention.'

The message is reasonably short in this case but some aspects might still be misunderstood so to end off we need to take the final step in effective communication.

Asking for action
The country parson, asked to explain the success of his sermons, confided his secret as 'First I tell them what I'm going to tell them; then I tell them; then I tell them what I told them.' School teachers, university lecturers and others whose results depend on their spoken words being understood and retained by their listeners will bear witness to the value of this method.

So, to make sure our message has been received and understood our final step is to ask for action. In doing so we repeat the important points we want to reinforce and make it quite clear what action we are asking for. Finally, we ask for confirmation of understanding.

When trying to confirm understanding it is important to ask open-ended questions, that is questions that cannot be answered by a simple 'Yes' or 'No'. Few of us like to admit that we haven't understood a message – particularly from a senior – so the temptation to reply 'Yes' when asked is very strong. If the question is open-ended we are forced to frame a reply which will indicate our understanding or lack of it.

'I liked your presentation. It went well. Have you ever thought how much easier you would find it to explain the complicated part in the middle if you used some well chosen slides?

If you will pick out the areas where you think they will help and do some rough sketches before Monday, I will get them made up professionally and get them back to you in time for your big presentation on Friday. That way there will be less chance of those important clients missing the message by not paying attention.

So if you'll give me your draft slides – not more than 20 – by 10am Monday I'll get them back to you before Friday. What's the latest I must get them to you for inclusion in your presentation?'

In that example we have only recorded the speaker's message but of course in practice the listener would be responding to each step of the approach, either verbally or non-verbally, indicating his/her agreement or otherwise.

That description of the process of effective communication, from deciding your objective through to confirming understanding, took us some time to go through but with a very little practice you will find you are applying it subconsciously whenever you have to communicate an important message. Certainly, if you do use the process, it will save you many hours of frustration waiting for things to happen which have been delayed by miscommunication.

Listening

We have spoken at length of how to communicate when you are initiating the process yourself but at least half the time you are on the receiving end of the process – you are the receiver not the sender. And this is the area where more than half of the miscommunication problems occur.

Studies measuring the retention of verbal messages have shown that, in subjects which are of direct interest to the listener, not more than 75 per cent is generally retained as measured immediately afterwards. Even this retention falls rapidly after a day or so. Where the subject is of personal concern, retention drops to 65 per cent and where it is only of general interest, 45 per cent is the maximum that can be expected.

So listening isn't something we can take for granted and if we want to avoid miscommunication we will have to work hard at it.

Creative Listening

1. Concentrate on the speaker – try to empty your mind of other thoughts.
2. Don't prejudge the message or jump to conclusions.
3. Don't interrupt the speaker.
4. Verify your version and make sure you understand before ending the discussion.

Watching the speaker is certainly a help in concentrating. When President Bush has something important to say he says, 'Read my lips', because he knows that is one way of ensuring concentration.

When we prejudge what a speaker is going to say it means we have been listening with only half our brain and using the other half to search our memory for similar inputs. Similarly, if we jump to conclusions it means we have switched off before the speaker has ended and are applying our own experiences to the situation described. In both cases we will not be listening to the message and may well miss some vital bits.

The same thing happens when we interrupt – we stop listening in order to frame what we are going to say. So apart from interrupting the thought process of the speaker which may cause a distorted message, we may well have missed part of what has been said.

If the person communicating with us has not read this book and adopted the method of communication we have been studying together, he/she may not take the steps necessary to ensure understanding. If so, it is up to us to do so by asking questions until we are quite sure we know what is meant.

Body language

One important point we haven't covered is the question of your personal attitude when communicating. This is known technically as non-verbal communication or body language and is the way in which you, deliberately or unknowingly, communicate your personality to the other party.

If you want others to do things for you or freely give you information, you must appear to them to be deserving of their help and co-operation. This means you have to appear pleasant, friendly and unthreatening in your manner as well as in your speech. If, on the other hand, you adopt a sergeant-majorish manner you can expect obedience but no help.

A detailed study of body language is beyond the purpose of this book but there are many excellent books on the subject and, if you seriously want to improve your communication skills, a little time spent reading one would be an investment.

Making meetings work

As we have said earlier, meetings are the arch-criminals in the miscommunication business, taking up and wasting probably more of your time than any other activity. Studies suggest that, in most businesses, between 40 and 75 per cent of management time is probably taken up in meetings of one sort and another. The same studies suggest that effective meetings may number as little as 25 per cent of the total. In other words, if you are in business, between 30 and 55 per cent of your committed time is currently being wasted in unproductive meetings. There are no statistics available for non-business situations but the proportion of truly effective meetings is probably about the same.

Committed Time

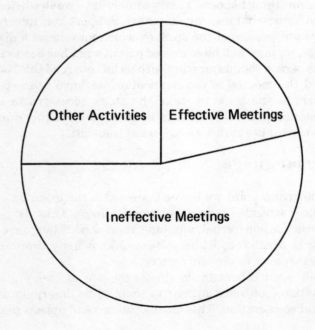

Cost of Meetings

Assuming that the true cost of an average employee is approximately twice his/her salary, the following equation will indicate the cost of a meeting per minute

$$\frac{S \times 2 \times N}{H}$$

Where S equals the average salary of those attending. N equals number attending. H equals the hours per working year.

On this basis the cost of a meeting of 10 middle executives would probably be in excess of £2.50 per minute.

On the basis of those figures meetings would appear to be an expensive luxury. Unfortunately, we can't get along without them because, for all their faults when badly run, they certainly can produce results if properly handled. Some of their principal advantages are:

- They help to pool expertise and to tap new sources
- They provide up-to-date knowledge of a situation
- They can capitalise on the synergy of team-working
- They provide an opportunity to encourage participation.

Meetings take many forms but generally fall into one of four main categories:

| Information | Decision-making | Team-building | Statutory |

Information meetings are held to disseminate information quickly and accurately to a number of people without running the risk of the 'line-loss' which distorts messages passed from person to person. They are also held to gather information from a number of sources, such as a report-back meeting on a campaign or project.

Decision-making meetings are held when the person responsible for the decision wants to obtain the views of others involved, help in solving a problem, and suggestions for alternative courses of action.

Team-building meetings are held to allow members to get help with their problems, to provide support for members, to encourage members to participate in the affairs of the team as, for example, church groups, women's groups or work groups of any kind.

Statutory meetings are those required by law or by the rules of an association. They are normally governed by rigid procedures and use a language foreign to the layperson which seems to have been specially designed to make it extremely difficult for anyone outside the executive to participate.

Apart from the last type of meeting about which you can do little except resign your seat as soon as possible, there are a number of ways in which the productivity of meetings can be improved and the drain on your time resource reduced.

Making Meetings Productive

1. Don't call a meeting If you can possibly avoid it by using some other sort of communication.
2. Before going any further define the objective of the meeting in writing. The more precise and measurable your objective the more likely you are to achieve it.
3. Choose the members of your meeting with care and due regard to their ability to contribute.
4. Choose a venue and time convenient to a majority of members.
5. Advise the members three days in advance of the objective, agenda, time and place, to allow them to do their own preparation.
6. Prepare yourself and any material you need to make the meeting productive and interesting. Consider any strong personalities among the participants who may need special handling and plan a strategy. Ensure there will be no interruptions.
7. Call the meeting to order as soon as possible, welcome the members and state the objective of the meeting as briefly as possible.
8. Stimulate the discussion by asking open-ended questions and ensuring there is no criticism of members' contributions until all views have been expressed.
9. Keep contributions short and to the point and do not allow any one person to dominate the discussion. Summarise the important points raised. Constantly repeat the objective to help members concentrate on the subject.

---

10. Thank all members for their contribution. Record agreement and action decided and circulate to all members.

Follow up on all decisions

If you can follow that outline next time you have to call a meeting you will be amazed at how much more productive, and thence more enjoyable, it will be. When a productive meeting ends the participants leave with a feeling of achievement and improved morale. When an unproductive meeting ends, as you probably know, the feeling is one of frustration and regret at the time wasted in pointless discussion.

But suppose you're not the chairperson, what can you do then to avoid wasting time at meetings?

Helping Meetings Work

1. Make sure you know the objective of the meeting and what contribution you are expected (or wish) to make.
2. Ask how long the meeting is planned to be and make only that time available.
3. Arrive on time and fully prepared.
4. Keep your contributions short and to the point.
5. If the discussion starts to wander off the subject tactfully draw the chairperson's attention to the fact.
6. When the agenda has been completed stand up and ask to be excused. If it is not completed in the allotted time, point this out to the chair and ask how much longer you will be required to attend as you have other matters to see to.
7. Make sure you get a copy of the minutes and take prompt action on anything affecting you.

There are many other forms of specialised communication that we haven't touched on which can also fall prey to miscommunication. Such specialised activities as negotiating, selling, counselling and disciplining are beyond the scope of this book. However, they all have one thing in common – they all require application of the basic method of effective communication as outlined at the beginning of this chapter. So, whatever your miscommunication problems, whether at work or at home, mastery of that simple method will help increase your productive use of time.

Points to remember

1. Communicating means to exchange information *and* understanding.
2. The first requirement of any communication process is the determination of a precise objective.
3. An effective method of communicating is to use the AIDA process which comprises four steps – Attention, Interest, Detail and Action.
4. The most effective way to gain attention is to refer to the other party's objectives.
5. Interest can be aroused by showing how the objectives may be affected by what you have to say.
6. The detail should include what, when, where, how and why.
7. Asking for the action required will confirm that the message has been understood.
8. Creative listening will ensure you understand messages passed to you from others.
9. Unproductive meetings can be wasting up to 55 per cent of your committed time.
10. Meetings can be made productive by applying 10 simple rules which advise you not to call a meeting if it can be avoided and to define the objective clearly before embarking on any meeting.

Chapter 7
Putting Your Plan into Action

Avoiding hi-intrusion at the office

When we said that up to 75 per cent of your time can be spent in meetings we were talking of meetings of all kinds, both formal and informal, involving several people or just two of you. All meetings intrude on your committed time in that, unless they are a part of your plan, they take up time you could be using for more personally productive activity. They are the very basis of hi-intrusion, the fifth of the progress-stoppers we listed in Chapter 3 which can make serious inroads into your committed time.

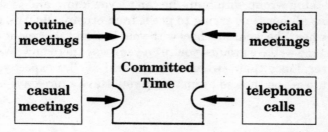

We have already suggested that you should avoid calling meetings if other forms of communication will do as good a job. However, what can you do about the meetings to which *you* are called? These normally fall into two categories – routine and special.

Routine meetings are those held on a regular basis – come hell or high water – usually to report back on ongoing activities. Often the information exchanged is stale and could easily be distributed in other ways which would not intrude on the time of those attending. If we were solely concerned with our personal productivity we would beg to be excused from many of them.

Unfortunately, we are often more concerned with such factors as status and office politics. Once we have achieved a certain rank, attendance at particular meetings is considered a visible sign to the rest of the world that we have arrived. Even if we had a legitimate reason for not attending, office politicians would quickly spread the word that we were out of favour – if not actually on the way out – if we failed to turn up. So we go on wasting valuable time in misguided efforts to protect our precarious standing. Perhaps when we have demonstrated the positive results of increased personal productivity such posturing will no longer be necessary.

Provided the subject is one which affects you and you have checked that your presence is vital, there is little you can do about the intrusion of *special meetings* except to follow the guidelines we have given for keeping them on track. The real problem lies in *casual meetings*.

'I do hope you don't mind my popping in like this. I saw your car outside so I knew you hadn't gone out. I wanted to tell you about that awful woman who's just moved in opposite – the one who dresses like a tramp and has a screechy laugh you could hear from here. Well it seems her husband has something wrong with him – he can't – you know, and so she spends all her time trying to get it from others. Oh! You do know her. She went to school with you. You and she belong to the same welfare group – you're on your way there now. Well I never, fancy that – what a small world. Well, I expect you want to get on then so I won't keep you. Have a nice day.'

Probably not all your casual meetings are as profitless as this example but nevertheless they can play havoc with a carefully planned day. Without retiring to a monastery, convent or desert island it's fairly hard to avoid them altogether, so how can we manage them so that they do as little damage as possible?

Avoiding Hi-intrusion

At the office:
1. Analyse all interruptions
    (a) Unavoidable
    (b) Avoidable
2. Develop definite responses to each type
3. Make appointments
4. Close the door
5. Stand up

Analysing your casual meetings over a short period of time will give you a valuable indication of where the fault lies – with you or with some other party. If you study the analysis honestly you will note that many of the avoidable meetings are a result of disorganisation or miscommunication. You have failed to delegate properly or you have failed to communicate fully, causing people to refer back to you matters which they should have been able to settle on their own.

Avoidable intrusions by seniors or colleagues are more difficult to handle. The boss who drops in on a 'walk-about' having read a book which says that you can manage by walking around instead of applying your brains to the problems in your in-tray. The colleague who is having trouble with her boyfriend and has to share it with someone or burst.

'Collecting material for a book on productivity, I visited many head offices and spent some time in their reception areas waiting for people who failed to keep to their agreed appointments.

To avoid wasting valuable time I used to keep a log of the time wasted by staff members who visited the telephonist/receptionists for a chat. My highest count was 10 minutes during a period of 15 minutes. That of course excluded the time they took to walk to and from the area and to settle down once they returned to their desks. That company was losing the equivalent of one employee's output every day. The executive was unhappy at having kept me waiting and even more discomforted when I told him the result of my research – he was probably used to chatting them up himself!'

Handling these casual callers without giving lasting offence is not easy but it is possible to make the interview unrewarding for the caller without actually being offensive. One well-used and successful method is to stand up as soon as they approach and remain standing until they go. If they ask you to sit, tell them that a short break standing will do your back good and 'I know you won't be long anyway, will you?'

This usually works well against all but the most hardened egotist. However, you will need to develop other strategies to keep the standing interview as short as possible. Keep your responses terse – a simple yes or no is sufficient. Don't use the opportunity to offload any of your problems. Let your body language indicate impatience and resentment at the intrusion – finger the papers on your desk, look at your watch every minute or so. With a little ingenuity you will find your stream of unproductive intrusions reduced to a trickle.

Controlling your own employees is a bit easier – all you have to do is to ask them to make prior appointments. If you tell them that the reason is that you want to brief yourself before seeing them so that you can make a worthwhile contribution to their problem they will admire your technique – and prepare themselves a little better in consequence. The appointment should be for a definite time-span, say five minutes, so that there is time only to discuss the business in hand.

Another classic way to avoid intrusion is to close your door and hang a notice on it which will deter all but the most determined intruder. Unfortunately, nowadays, few of us have doors to close and it's quite hard to withdraw in an open-plan office. However, with some applied thought it can be done by changing the direction of your work station, becoming immersed in your PC terminal when you spot invaders, removing spare chairs from your area or even moving partitions and cabinets.

Many large organisations recognise this problem and institute a 'quiet hour', morning and afternoon, when it is understood that no visits or casual meetings take place.

Avoiding hi-intrusion at home

For those of us who work at home either at a business, a hobby or running a household and bringing up a family, intrusion can be just as disturbing if we let it break into our planned activities.

How often have you heard someone complain, 'I just wasn't able to get anything done today. It was just one thing after another. First the woman next door wanting to borrow my scissors – she'd lost hers. Then a woman from the library about overdue books. Then the garden service and by then I had to fetch the kids – the whole morning wasted.'

Avoiding Hi-intrusion
At home:
1. Analyse all interruptions
(a) Unavoidable
(b) Avoidable
2. Install an answering machine
3. Install a door microphone
4. Keep it brief
5. Stand up

Here again you should analyse all interruptions into those which are unavoidable – repairmen, friends and family – and those which are avoidable such as canvassers, beggars etc.

How you handle the first category – unavoidable callers – will depend very much on their value to you. Repairmen can usually be persuaded to make appointments – unless it's a disaster. Friends and family are usually understanding enough to recognise when you are busy, especially if you make it obvious by continuing your work. An invitation to a meal at a later and more convenient date will probably heal any damage done by your coolness.

The best way to prevent interruption by the second sort of avoidable intruder is to erect mechanical barriers. Install a telephone answering machine which can protect you from unwanted phone calls. Consider installing an entry microphone so that callers have to announce themselves before being admitted, thus giving you the opportunity to decide your strategy before coming face to face with them. Many households have such systems installed for security purposes but you will find it equally valuable in screening out avoidable intrusions into your planned activities.

When you do decide to meet either type of intrusion, plan to keep the interview as brief and to the point as possible and call on the techniques we mentioned before such as standing up, looking at your watch etc. If you are really pressed, set the timer in the kitchen to go off after three minutes, giving you an excuse to end the conversation to attend to some fictitious chore or other.

Managing your telephone

The final, and perhaps the most insidious, intruder we have to manage is our telephone which can wreck the most carefully laid work plan but without which many of us cannot work. How do we manage without throwing it out of the window in frustration?

Of course, the ideal is to have an intermediary to answer it for you and filter the calls, passing on only those you have previously authorised. Unfortunately, not all of us have assistants or secretaries, so what can we do?

One way is to install a telephone answering machine. You can either let it record all incoming calls and reply at your convenience or you can listen to whoever is calling and answer only those which are unavoidable and urgent. Either way you will be spared many of the nuisance calls you waste time on now.

If you can't get mechanical help you'll have to develop a technique for handling telephone interruptions which will fall into the same categories as the other casual intrusions we talked of earlier. Obviously, standing up won't help much but keeping to the point will.

——— ◊ ———

'If you want a real blow to your ego get hold of one of those microphones which fit on to a telephone and record your conversations for a day or so. When you have time, play them back and listen to the nonsense, the repetition and the time-wasting that go on. How many times did you say goodbye without ringing off? How long did it take you to stop talking about the weather and get to the point? How many of the calls were really necessary? How many achieved your objective?'

——— ◊ ———

If the call is unavoidable or one you want to receive try to keep it as brief as possible. Make notes as you listen so that you won't have to ask for a repeat. Keep it tight and to the point and don't spend a lot of time on unnecessary pleasantries (unless it's your best customer). If the call is avoidable and you don't want to waste time on it at that point simply say that you are tied up and will call back later. Fix a time and ring off.

One of the worst aspects of telephone interruptions is the length of time it takes you to get back to what you were doing before. If you did a study with a stop-watch you would find it taking you anything up to half a minute before you can pick up where you left off. That's not much on its own but if you multiply it by 20 calls a day it's almost an hour a week or two days a year!

Getting away from it all

No matter how effective the barriers you erect there comes a time when the importance and urgency of some task demands your unbroken concentration. At such a time the only thing to do is to move off somewhere where you will not be disturbed by anyone – a special office or room, an hotel, a country cottage. Even a long distance train or plane journey can provide welcome isolation at present, although they are talking of installing satellite telephones which will destroy even those havens.

Getting it right first time

Fifty years ago grandmother used to say, 'Prevention is better than cure' when she administered a dose of castor oil, presumably inferring that a healthy stomach would give less trouble than an unhealthy one and the cost of achieving it was negligible. It's taken us a long time to recognise the truth of her saying and to recognise the enormous cost of misapplication of resources in terms of productivity both at home and in business.

Today the key word is 'quality', meaning the degree of perfection which satisfies all a customer's requirements – 'customer' being used in its broadest sense as the end user of a product or service we produce at home or at work (rather than simply a purchaser). Acceptable 'quality' can be defined and specified for each particular user. Products or services which do not meet specification have to be scrapped or reworked, in either case involving a complete waste of the resources used originally to produce them.

'I've always considered myself handy with a saw and hammer around the house, but I'm afraid the results of my handiwork always had a rather patchy look about them and I had to do a lot of making good where I had drilled holes in the wrong place or sawn a bit of wood the wrong length.

One day, in the pub, I met a joiner who told me he worked a lot with valuable hard woods. I told him about my problems and asked him how much he had to scrap when he worked. "Oh," he said, "I could never scrap anything – I'd get the sack. No, my father taught me never to cut or mark anything until I had measured it at least three times and got the same answer. That way I find I don't have to do anything over."

Since I followed his advice the quality of my work has improved enormously and I seldom waste material by bad cutting or drilling. It must have saved me quite a bit of money – apart from the hair I used to tear out in frustration!'

In those days dedication to quality was restricted to craftsmen and the rest of us were dedicated to churning out quantity rather than quality in an endeavour to keep prices down. Nowadays 'quality' is all-important and strangely enough, quality production saves so much waste of resources that in the end it is more economical than the old way of doing things.

This may sound hard to believe because taking extra care and time and using better materials and methods will cost money. But when you add up the total, the reduction in waste more than compensates for the extra cost, leaving some over for extra profit.

% of Production Costs				
10	**Prevention**			
10	**Measurement**		15	**Prevention**
15	**Rejects**		5	**Measurement**
			0	**Rejects**
35%			20%	

Reduction = 15%

Those figures are broad averages for industries that have changed their approach to quality but the same benefits await you as an individual because, unless you are a most unusual person, you make mistakes and have to do things again. The only difference is that you don't add up the cost in terms of the resources you have wasted – principally your own time and whatever machines or materials you use. Maybe you should.

- Do I have a standard by which I judge my output?
- Do I reach that standard – always? Most times? Sometimes?
- What could I do to improve the quality of my output?
- What would be the benefits – to me? To others?

The answer to the first question should be easy if you have set yourself objectives and standards as we discussed a couple of chapters ago. And the answer to the second will come from the review of your action plans.

How you can improve the quality of your output will depend entirely on what occupation you are measuring. If you are producing something tangible you will know how its quality can be improved or you can ask your supervisor what standard is expected and how you can reach it. If you are a manager or supervisor your output is the output of those you manage – the better you manage them the greater their output. Maybe a refresher course or a couple of books on management would give you some new ideas for improving the quality of your management. Certainly, applying some of the principles we have discussed together in this book will help considerably.

If you work at home you may not have thought about setting formal standards although you will probably have some subconscious ones. You might find it helpful to define them more accurately and to measure your performance against them – particularly how your 'customers' feel about them. Once that is achieved you can decide what you can do to improve the quality of your output.

As to what benefits you can expect you will certainly gain achievement satisfaction from producing a perfect product and will receive recognition, if not reward, from your customers. At the same time you will know that you are using your resources as productively as possible and thus moving towards one or other of your personal objectives, which, after all is what this is all about, isn't it?

Points to remember

1. Meetings, routine, casual and special, together with telephone calls, are the principal causes of hi-intrusion.
2. It will help you to avoid hi-intrusion at work if you analyse all

  interruptions over a week and classify them as either avoidable or unavoidable.
3. The need for avoidable meetings should be eliminated by better delegation and communication.
4. Techniques for reducing the impact of unavoidable meetings can be developed.
5. The same techniques can be adapted to reduce hi-intrusion in the home.
6. Installing an answering machine and improving your response technique are two ways to reduce the intrusion of telephone calls.
7. Quality may be defined as the degree of perfection which satisfies all the customer's requirements.
8. Producing a quality product is the most resource efficient way of combating misapplication.
9. Producing a quality product, whether in the office or home, will give you recognition, reward and personal satisfaction as well as help you towards your personal objectives.

Chapter 8
Self-Assessment

So far we have seen the importance of having clear, measurable objectives, a simple plan to achieve them and well-organised resources to enable us to carry out the plan. And we have seen how the 'progress-stoppers' can prevent or hinder our progress towards our objectives by forcing us to waste time in non-productive activity.

You'll remember that in Chapter 2 we talked about the two factors which affected productivity, namely, utilisation and efficiency – utilisation being the degree to which we make effective use of the resources available and efficiency being the speed and accuracy with which we do the work. You'll also remember we talked about the '4Ms' – money, manpower, materials and machinery – which are the resources we use in business (and in the home too).

When we talk about 'time' and 'time management' what we are really meaning is the utilisation of our personal manpower resource. This is measured in 'manhours' – one manhour representing one man or woman employed in some activity or other for one hour. So when we talk loosely about 'wasting time' what we really mean in terms of productivity is 'under utilising our personal manpower resource', ie, getting less output per manhour of our personal time than we should be.

Utilisation of materials

The same two factors also affect the productivity of the other resources – money, materials and machinery. Their productivity in real terms depends on how much and how well we use them. Money is the resource which enables us to obtain all the others and so we will be looking at it in detail later. But not all of us are conscious of the need to conserve materials and to use them efficiently, especially when they are scarce or costly.

A drought brings home to us graphically how much water we normally waste without thinking and how much better it can be used with a little care and thought. An imbalance of foreign trade emphasises the need to recycle paper and metals, materials we normally waste quite happily.

Materials Purchased				
Wasted			Used	
lost	damaged	surplus	wrongly	effectively

In most situations some of the materials purchased are never used. They are lost (or stolen), damaged in handling or over-ordered. Even some of those actually used are used wrongly, only the balance remaining being used effectively and productively. In most manufacturing businesses the wastage of materials purchased is estimated at more than 15 per cent; in service businesses more than 10 per cent of the materials are never used.

Exercising control over waste doesn't mean being niggardly or miserly. It simply means giving some thought to extracting the maximum use from the items you purchase. One way, as we said in the last chapter, is to buy 'quality' products and learn to use them effectively. Budgeting, or setting standards of consumption, is another way of focusing attention on the materials you use (which we will look at in Chapter 9).

In the meantime here is a simple review you can make of your present use of materials which may give you some ideas as to how to use them more productively.

My expenditure on materials (food, clothing, groceries, stationery, maintenance materials etc.) last month was

£

If I wasted 10 per cent of this by poor utilisation it would be

£

In fact I estimate that I wasted £   made up of the following items:

This month I will take the following action to improve utilisation:

If you carry out a simple review of your utilisation of materials like this once in a while you will be surprised how much waste you will uncover and, hopefully, avoid in future.

Utilisation of machinery

The term 'machinery' is used to cover all the other bits and pieces you need to operate a business or a home – machines, cars, trucks, offices, computers, furniture and so on. All of these cost money – some a great deal – and this investment is wasted when they are not being used to capacity.

Delivery company A buys a delivery van for £20,000 and depreciates it over five years. It travels 10,000 miles pa.

Its basic costs per year =   Its running costs =
   Depreciation   £4000   25p per mile
   Licence   £ 400   Its annual running costs over
   Insurance   £ 600   10,000 miles =
TOTAL pa   £5000   £2500

Its total cost per mile = $\dfrac{5000 + 2500}{10,000}$ = 75p per mile

Delivery company B buys the same van and has the same basic costs of £5000 per annum. It travels 20,000 miles per annum at 25p per mile for a total of £5000.

Its total costs are thus $\dfrac{5000 + 5000}{20,000}$ = 50p per mile

Which company would you choose to deliver your goods?

Of course the answer to that question is 'the company that gave the best value, ie quality for price' but on the face of it Company B has a head start because it is getting better utilisation from its vehicles. The figures in that example are not necessarily accurate in detail but they are near enough to illustrate the point and to make you think about the utilisation of some of your 'machinery'.

Nowadays, capital equipment is so costly that it is often more economical to hire what you need when you need it rather than to buy and have it standing idle. Because of this a whole new industry has sprung up which will hire (or lease) you anything you need – from a pair of garden shears to a fully equipped factory.

Personal resources

But we have other resources which we draw on every day and which don't fall under the '4Ms'. These are our personal resources comprising the '3As' – attributes, assets and associations. Few of us think about them and even fewer try to make them contribute productively to the attainment of our personal objectives.

'When he was five, Peter went with his father on a week-long fishing trip, camping overnight in quite a wild part of the country. He acquired an abiding love of fishing and was given his first rod at the age of eight. Thereafter, every spare day was spent fishing some river or hole for whatever he could lure to his rod and all his pocket money went on tackle.

Needless to say, his school work took second place and, when he left, his name was bottom of the list of pupils who passed. However, he was very good with his hands and got a job helping out in a local sports shop which specialised in fishing gear. Fairly soon he was handling all the rod repairs and started to get quite a reputation for the excellence of his work.

He noticed that most of the more expensive rods he handled were imported and wondered why they couldn't be made locally. One day he mentioned this to his girlfriend who worked in a local bank. "Why don't you make them, Peter?" she asked. "You're good with your hands and you know as much about rods as anyone."

"I only wish I could," he countered. "But what would I use for money to buy all the material and gear I would need?"

"Well, you could use your savings and you could try the bank," she said. "I know the manageress in charge of the Small Business Section well – I'm sure she would help if I asked her."

Next day he saw the manageress who was impressed by his scheme and managed to help him get a sizeable loan to start up a small business making high quality specialised rods in the garage at his father's house.

That was some years ago and since then his name has become a household word in the fishing fraternity. Now he has his own premises but he still does it all himself, taking a couple of weeks to finish a rod and charging an arm and a leg for it. I have had my name down for one of his rods for three months and will probably have to wait another three before I can experience the joy of its craftsmanship.'

In that true example, Peter used all his personal resources to achieve his objective. His *attributes* included his knowledge and skill in handling and repairing rods and his strong motivation to get on in spite of doing badly at school. His *assets* included his savings and his father's garage, while his *association* with his girlfriend provided valuable advice, and her association with her colleague made the whole project feasible.

How can you use more of your personal resources to help you, too, achieve your objectives? As with any resources the first step is to determine just what you've got before you can think about putting them to work.

Attributes

The best way to review your attributes is to write yourself a curriculum vitae, or CV as it is more generally known. A CV is designed to tell potential employers who you are and what you can do – a form of personal advertisement. Like all advertisements there's quite a knack in writing an effective CV but you'll find it relatively easy if you remember that the other party is more interested in *what you can do* than in *what you are* or have been.

So you start off by listing your achievements – the successful things you have been responsible for in your life to date. List the latest ones first and then go back as far as you can. At this stage don't exclude any because you think they are too unconnected – they may spur you to think of ways in which your experience could be adapted to less exotic ends.

The next step is to list your work experience, job by job. Then come your educational achievements ending up with your outside interests (if these are publishable!).

If you study your new CV carefully you will experience two things. First, you will find your morale considerably lifted by reading about all the good things you have achieved but had forgotten about, and second, you will see many areas of expertise or interest that you are not currently putting to productive use. These are the attributes you can call on to help you achieve your objectives.

Personal development
At the beginning of this book we asked you to list your objectives under three headings – at work, at home and personal development. If you glance back at that list you may find that some of the items you wrote under that last heading, personal development, bear little relation to the record of your CV and you may find it helpful to analyse your strengths and weaknesses and reassess your objectives in the light of your findings.

Personal Resources Analysis		
Resource	**Strength**	**Weakness**
Knowledge		
Experience		
Skill		
Health		
Appearance		
Motivation		
Action required to build on strengths:		
Action required to strengthen weaknesses:		

Assets

Similarly you can list your assets and their current values. Studying that list will tell you whether they are being fully used in the attainment of your objectives or could be more productive used in some other way.

Analysis of Assets			
Asset	**Value**	**% Time used**	**Productivity**
Action to improve productivity:			

Associations

They say, 'It's not *what* you know, it's *who* you know that counts in the end.' This may sound cynical but unfortunately, like all such sayings, there's more than a grain of truth in it. Your family, friends, colleagues and acquaintances all have attributes, assets and associations which can be of assistance to you and, in most cases, they would be more than willing to help where they can. But it's up to you to determine exactly how to put this extremely valuable resource to work.

Many people hold back from using their associations in this way, perhaps feeling that they are taking advantage of them. But there is a substantial difference between using your associations to help you to reach your objectives, or networking as it is known, and simple, old-fashioned 'sponging'.

In the first case people will help you because they know they will be repaid, not necessarily in material terms but more often in an enrichment of your association. They also know you will do your bit to help them to the best of your ability should they need it. This is how a network operates – by mutual support.

93

Sponging, on the other hand, is a one-way operation where you receive without giving in return and is justifiably shunned by most independent people.

So, while you are making action lists, think about your associations and record the strength or potential of each one to help you reach your objective. And, having listed them, make sure you keep the relationship alive and well by phoning, corresponding or meeting from time to time.

Family life
If you are lucky enough to form part of a family then this can be the basis for the strongest support group of all. However, like networking, it won't develop unless you earn it.

As a starting point it would do no harm to analyse the strengths and weaknesses of your family relationships and think about how to build on the one and buttress the other. Families without relationship problems are rare (and very lucky) and there doesn't seem to be any universal formula for achieving sound relationships.

However, one thing is clear, and that is that such problems seriously affect the productivity of all the parties involved. So if you are unlucky enough to have such a problem, resolving it should be one of your priority objectives.

Even if you have no such problem there is likely to be some clash between the priority objectives of your work life and those of your home and family. This issue can only be decided with the consensus of those concerned, whose decision should be based on their unemotional assessment as to which course of action will best help you to achieve all of your objectives. Which is easy to say but quite difficult to achieve.

This exercise could well change some of the objectives on the list you prepared in Chapter 1 and possibly suggest some more productive use for the discretionary time you currently spend away from work. Combined with the other analyses we have suggested it could open your eyes as to the wealth of your personal resources.

Points to remember

1. Time management means the utilisation of our personal manpower resource.
2. Whether we are at work or at home we have four types of

tangible resources – the '4Ms', money, manpower, materials, machinery.

3. Controlling waste will improve the utilisation of materials.
4. Investment in 'machinery' is wasted unless it is used to its full capacity.
5. We also have a number of personal resources – the '3As', attributes, assets and associations.
6. The best way to review your attributes is to write a CV detailing your achievements, experience and education.
7. An analysis of your assets will tell you how productively they are being used.
8. Your associations are a most important resource which can help you achieve your objectives.
9. Your most powerful association could be your family.

Chapter 9
Money is the Root . . .

Whether or not love of money is the root of all evil, money is certainly a very necessary evil, particularly these days. Over the last 6000 years it has taken the place of barter as the medium of exchange used in buying and selling, mainly because of its ease of handling. A pocketful of money takes up much less room than a flock of sheep when you want to buy something at the market.

Money in itself has no real existence; it is only a promise that the governor of the national bank will pay the bearer a specified sum of money. In fact, he never does but his 'promises' can be exchanged for other goods and services. The value of his 'promises' varies according to how people see his ability to meet them. If they rate this highly their value increases and people will buy more goods. On the other hand, if they don't think he will be able to keep his promises their value decreases until, as has happened in some third world countries, they become almost valueless.

What is money?

Do you see it as an end in itself – the pot of gold waiting for you at the end of the rainbow? Is its acquisition all-important – your overriding objective? Or is it simply a means to an end – the necessary evil you need to achieve your objectives?

However you see it, money is simply a resource – the last of the '4Ms'. Indeed, it is our most important resource because we can exchange it for all the other tangible resources we need to meet our objectives and, sometimes, for some of the intangible ones as well. We have seen how the way we use our other resources affects our ability to achieve our objectives. Money is no different from any other resource; you can use it productively to help you reach your objectives or you can waste it.

Total Money Available		
Tax 25%	Wasted 10%	Used productively 65%

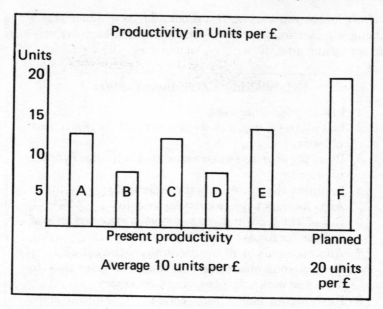

Zero-base budgeting

In order to overcome this problem and to enable the production of dynamic and realistic budgets the 'Zero-base' method was developed in the USA in the early 1970s, originally for the state of Georgia under Jimmy (later President) Carter.

There are three fundamentals in zero-base budgeting:

1. Every expenditure item must be described and justified in detail.
2. Each item must be ranked in order of priority based on its productivity and contribution to overall objectives.
3. Available funds must be allocated strictly according to these priorities.

Although this method was developed for a civil service organisation, it has subsequently been widely accepted by progressive businesses as the only way to produce meaningful budgets which can ensure that available funds are allocated to the most productive operations.

Because of its orientation towards objectives and productivity it is also an ideal way in which to plan and organise the use of your own personal money resource. It creates a self-imposed discipline

99

which forces you constantly to consider your objectives when using or allocating your money resource. It is also relatively easy to set up and administer.

Establishing a Zero-base Budget

1. List all your objectives.
2. List all the things you do or want to do to reach your objectives.
3. Place the objectives and associated activities in order of priority.
4. Estimate their annual cost (realistically).
5. Add the costs to get a cumulative total.
6. Cut off the list when you reach your expected level of income (or funds).
7. Allocate funds to all the items above the cut-off.
8. Review your objectives and priorities from time to time and make changes where necessary.
9. Review your expenditure constantly and take steps to stay within your budget limits.
10. If you can save on estimated expenditure you can consider the next item below the cut-off.

That may look like a rather formidable list but in practice it is easy to do – the only difficult part you will find being establishing priorities. If you are dealing with a family budget it's essential to get the family members' agreement to the final priorities.

In the following example of how a family might set up a zero-base budget to help them manage their money resource we have included all expenses, including everyday living expenses.

Smith Family Budget				
Priority	**Planned activity**	**Objective**	**Annual cost**	
			Actual	**Cumulative**
1.	Mortgage payments	Security	6000	6000
2.	Living expenses	Subsistence	4500	10,500
3.	Running 2nd car	Mobility	1200	11,700
4.	Entertainment	Networking	1500	13,200
5.	Life insurance	Security	1200	14,400
6.	New kitchen shelves	Improve assets	1500	15,900

7.	Holiday timeshare	Relaxation	600	16,500
8.	Annual holiday	Relaxation	1200	17,700
9.	Repairs/redecorate	Maintain assets	600	18,300
10.	Replace clothing Self	Appearance	1000	19,300
	Spouse		1000	20,300
	Family		600	20,900
11.	Golf club, self	Relaxation/	1200	22,100
	Tennis, spouse	Networking	700	22,800
=======	====================	===================	==============
12.	Video recorder	Family life	1000	23,800
13.	Hire of videos	Family life	250	24,050
14.	New car	Improve assets	2400	26,450

In the above example the family's net income was £23,000 so the cut-off line came after item 11 and before item 12. If they thought the video recorder was essential, they would either have to find a way of buying or leasing it for less than £200 per year or else change the priority of something else. Of course, if Mr Smith got a rise in salary or won a prize competition they might be able to move the line downwards. But the important point is that they would know what to spend the extra income on to meet their objectives.

You may not agree with their objectives or priorities but the principle of planning the productive use of your money resource in this way remains sound and practical. If you have not tried this sort of exercise before your first attempts to budget and to stick to it may not be very successful. However, if you persevere you will soon start to benefit from it and that reward in itself will be sufficient to keep you working at it.

Whether you use the fixed-base or zero-base method of budgeting you will need to keep records of your expenditure so that you can measure your progress as you go through the year. This doesn't mean a complicated set of account books but simply keeping receipts of your cash purchases, a copy of the voucher if you pay by credit card and completing the counterfoil if you pay by cheque.

When you receive your monthly statement you can check each item and pencil in what it was for. On the reverse side you can pencil in details of the cash receipts for that month after which you can throw them away and simply keep the statements which will give you all the information you need to monitor your progress against your budget.

Matching income and expenditure

Costing out your plans in this way will bring home to you the adequacy or otherwise of your present money resource to meet the objectives you have set for yourself. If it is adequate then you are either a very lucky person or you have already learned how to keep both objectives and resources in balance, which is the secret so simply explained by Charles Dickens' Mr Micawber in his oft-quoted formula

> 'Income twenty pounds, expenditure nineteen pounds nineteen and sixpence equals happiness. Income twenty pounds, expenditure twenty pounds and sixpence equals misery.'

In those days the answer was relatively simple – if you wanted a happy life you 'cut your coat according to the cloth' you had available; you stayed within your means or you ended up in the extreme discomfort of a debtors' prison. Today, when aspirations are rising daily, encouraged by the media, and easy money appears to be available for the asking, it's not so easy to temper your objectives to the reality of your finite resources. So where do you start?

If you were faced with a situation in business where there appeared to be insufficient funds to do what you wanted to do, you would normally be required to carry out a feasibility study, that is a detailed examination of the situation.

Feasibility Study

1. What do I really want to achieve?
2. When must it be done or completed?
3. How is it to be done? (plan)
4. Are there any alternative methods of achieving it?
5. What will each method cost?
6. Which is the cheapest acceptable method?
7. When will the money be required?
8. What is my revised objective?

The first question asks you to challenge your objective. What do you really want to achieve? Sometimes, when we formulate our objectives, we can get a bit starry eyed and divorced from reality.

So it's helpful to go back and make quite sure what it is you want.

Suppose you have your mind set on a new car. Do you really need a new car or are you simply tired of the unreliability of the old one, in which case your objective is to obtain a reliable means of transport, not necessarily a new car?

The answer to the question 'When must it be done?' will obviously depend on how badly your present objectives are being affected by the unreliability of your transport. It is important to specify a date otherwise you are likely to put it off day by day.

How do you propose to buy the new car? Trade in the old one as a deposit on a hire purchase contract? Sell the old one privately and then use the money as a deposit? Cash in your savings and buy it outright? Get an overdraft from the bank? It is not our purpose to advise you which is the least costly option – there are many handy books which can help you – we merely want you to be aware of some of the many alternatives available when you make your decision.

But before you choose any of them you should ask yourself if there are any alternative ways of achieving your objective which you have now amended to 'Equipping myself with reliable transport'. When you state it like that there are many alternative ways of meeting it. Repairing the present car. Complete overhaul of the present car. Hiring a new car. Leasing a new car. Changing your job to one which provides transport. Joining a lift club. And so on.

Before you can make a decision you will need to cost out each alternative carefully and assess its effect on your money resource over the next year. This will enable you to decide which is the least costly, but still acceptable, method of meeting your objective.

Now, before you can make a decision, you will need to know when the money involved in your chosen method will be required so you can check on the possibility of meeting the cost by your chosen means. When must the action be taken or completed? If action is not required for some time you may be able to make a plan to find the resources required.

Finally, you can make your decision, state your revised objective and allocate it a priority in your budget.

Having been through that process with us you may well be saying, 'There's nothing new in that – we always thoroughly discuss any major purchase or investment before we go ahead.' And no doubt you do. However, the point we want to make is that, while you may discuss whether or not to take a particular line of action, you probably don't consider *all* the alternatives and their possible effect on your money resource.

'Once we have an idea of some action we want to take, it tends to grow in our minds until it dominates our thinking to such an extent that we quite literally "can't see the wood for the trees".

This can lead us to the situation where we develop excellent solutions to the wrong problems, a situation that occurs with alarming frequency in business.

Carrying out a proper investigation of a problem before defining it and then developing as many alternative solutions as possible before choosing the one that will best achieve your objective probably takes a bit longer but it is time well spent. Particularly when the problem affects your money resource.'

Increasing income and decreasing expenditure

If, having analysed your objectives thoroughly and committed yourself to their achievement, you then find that you have insufficient funds to meet their cost, what do you do? Well, you have two chances, as they say. You must either increase your income or decrease your expenditure, which is easy to say but more difficult to practise.

You can increase your income in a variety of ways. By using your new knowledge of personal productivity to help you to get a better job, if you are employed, or getting one if you are not. Using your spare time more productively to earn money – part-time work or working at home. There is a strong trend today towards the employment of part-timers working at home, particularly if you have a computer and can use it. You could even start up your own small business.

When her husband, Pete, was moved to a small country town, Alice was forced to give up her job at the dress shop where she had been for some years. She didn't mind so much because she was expecting their first child and would have had to stop work quite soon anyway.

104

In his new job Pete didn't get any overtime, and this, coupled with the loss of her excellent salary, meant that they had a good deal less to live on than before. Living expenses were a bit lower so they managed all right, but there wasn't much to spare to save for the overseas holiday they had been planning for almost a year.

After the baby arrived, Alice's time was taken up looking after her and making a comfortable home in the old house they had found. But after a while she had got on top of it and found she had a lot of time on her hands. She wondered what she could do to use her spare time and bring in some more money without neglecting the baby.

She had attended a course in dress design when she was at the shop and had learned dressmaking from her mother years before. She asked around the town and found that there was only one dressmaker who seemed to be kept very busy with alterations and didn't tackle any serious dressmaking.

She worked out what it would cost to buy a second-hand machine and a large table for cutting out, as well as the cost of advertising in the local paper and putting up a notice in the local draper's shop. Then she worked out what she could charge for making up a dress from a pattern and estimated how many she could handle in a month. When she had finished, she put her plan to Pete and asked him to agree to her drawing on their small savings account to buy what she needed. He agreed somewhat reluctantly, persuaded by the prospect of reviving their holiday plans.

As might be expected, business was slow to start with but after three months she had all the work she could manage and had started to build quite a reputation for high quality work. In a year they had enough saved to take their planned trip – but she didn't stop there. Now she's saving to buy more equipment to set up a small workshop in the garage to make special orders for her old employers in the city.

What are they going to do with the money? They want to save it to pay for a university education for the little girl – her mother doesn't want her to have to sew dresses on the dining room table just to go on a holiday!

That was an example of people using their personal resources to build up their money resource, thus making it possible for them to gain their objective and even consider a much longer-term one. They fitted their income to their aspirations.

Sometimes it just isn't possible to increase your income and then the only way to provide the money to meet your objectives is to reduce expenditure on other activities. This is often not as difficult as it looks at first.

Parkinson's Law, 'work expands to fill the time available', can also be applied to our income. 'Expenditure rises to meet income' is probably just as apt as the well known quotation, and just as common in practice. Of course, some of the rise in expenditure is due to inflation and there is little we can do about it. But not all.

There is no doubt that when times are easy we get into free spending habits and when they tighten up so do we. The trick is to reverse the natural order, like the multi-millionaire who, when asked the secret of his success said, 'When people are running, I walk, and when they are walking, I run like hell!'

Strict control of your expenditure in good times will result in some surplus funds which can be saved until times are bad (and costs therefore lower) when it will go further towards achieving your chosen objective. Strict control doesn't mean becoming a Scrooge. All it requires is that you consider each expenditure in the light of its contribution towards your all-important objectives.

One of the less obvious ways in which most of us waste money is in the payment of the inescapable items of expenditure such as mortgage, insurance, taxes and other levies. In this area we often take the line of least resistance and take whatever is offered without going too closely into the fine print, perhaps overlooking the unfortunate fact that there can be a great deal of difference between the cost of good and bad arrangements.

There are many handy books on the subject of arranging your personal finances which will help you to improve your position and save money in the long run. However, unless you are a do-it-yourself fanatic it is well worth getting professional advice from a qualified source such as an accountant or your banker. The investment you make in their charges may well prove to be the best you ever made.

Points to remember

1. Money is a resource like any other which can be used productively to help you reach your objectives or be simply wasted.
2. Plans to use the money resource are known as budgets – either 'fixed-base' or 'zero-base'.
3. To draw up a zero-base budget it is necessary to list your objectives and planned activities in priority order before allocating funds to them.
4. You cannot budget with either method without maintaining a record of your expenditure.
5. Before you include any major new item in your budget you should complete a feasibility study.
6. You can often make more productive use of your personal resources to increase your income to meet a particular objective.
7. A careful study of expenditure and strict adherence to a budget will often enable you to reduce expenditure.

Chapter 10
Where Do We Go From Here?

Personal audit

The answer to that question depends very much on where you are at present and how well you have been able to keep up with the various exercises we have suggested. It may help you to answer the question if we first review the main points we have covered together.

The principal theme running through this book has been the inescapable link between productivity and objectives. Without objectives productivity measurements are meaningless and without productivity the objectives are unobtainable.

That was why we started out by asking you to write down your personal objectives under three headings – at work, at home and personal development. From time to time we have suggested you might want to amend them in the light of what you had learned about yourself and your present productivity. Perhaps it will help you to do this objectively if you first ask yourself some searching personal questions and answer them honestly.

So before we go on, take a little time to answer the personal productivity audit below.

Personal Productivity Audit	A	B
(*A = Satisfactory, B = Could improve*)		
1. I have completed a time log		
2. I have reduced idle time to the minimum possible		
3. I have adequate time for family/personal objectives		
4. I have reduced wasted time below 10 per cent		
5. I have minimised interruptions		
6. My personal environment is tidy and functional		

7. I have delegated all work I don't have to do personally
8. I have introduced completed staff work
9. I have mastered the use of AIDA in communicating
10. I have reduced my involvement in formal/ informal meetings to a minimum
11. I am consciously producing a 'quality' product
12. Wastage of materials for which I am responsible has been eliminated
13. My 'machinery resources' are fully utilised
14. I am exploiting all my 'personal attributes'
15. My personal 'assets' are fully utilised
16. I am developing my 'associations'
17. I have drawn up a realistic budget
18. I am adhering to my budget
19. I have defined precise objectives for myself
    at work
    at home
    personal development
20. I have set standards by which to measure my progress towards my objectives

Your action plan

Any item which you have shown as 'Could improve' will have to be translated into a measurable objective and added to your list. If you now rewrite all of these as critical results which you have to achieve (as discussed in Chapter 5) you can draw up an action plan to achieve them all.

My Personal Action Plan			
No	Critical result	Action required	Timing

Remember that the critical result must include a standard of measurement (quantity, quality, cost and/or time) and must include times of commencement and completion. Unless you pin yourself down to these essentials you will never 'find the time' to start them and won't be able to measure progress towards their completion.

When you enter the 'timing' you will have to develop some sort of priority for each activity and you can reflect this in the 'No' column. You must decide the basis for your priority listing – whether it is to be urgency, importance, profitability, ease of accomplishment or whatever. There is always a temptation to do the easy ones first, which is fine if they also qualify on other grounds and make a major contribution to your objectives. If not you should resist the temptation and buckle down to tackling the more important, urgent or profitable ones.

Resources

Once you have a clear plan of action you will need to check that you have the resources to carry it out – remember the 4 Rights – the right amount of the right resource in the right place at the right time.

When considering your resources don't forget to delegate wherever you can. Remember, even complicated jobs contain some simple components which can be 'fragmented' out and given to someone less skilled to do, thus releasing more of your time for the more complicated and profitable activities.

Don't forget the money

If your answer to item 18 in the personal productivity audit indicated a need for action, this should also be translated into a critical result and included in your action plan together with any projects for which you need to accumulate funds.

Review your plan

Drawing up your objectives and action plan may have seemed like a lot of work, but putting the plan into action requires much more which you may tend to shelve unless you discipline yourself to review the plan regularly. And, having reviewed it, take action to bring into line any CRs that are lagging behind their target dates.

It isn't all drudgery by any means because, as you see yourself making progress towards your objectives, your sense of real personal accomplishment will more than compensate for the effort you put into achieving it.

As you review the plan you may want to change some of the objectives in the light of developments which have taken place since you drew it up. This is quite normal and any dynamic plan will undergo changes before it is completed. Provided the changes are for the better no harm will be done, but you should try to avoid scrapping objectives and/or plans simply because they are difficult to accomplish.

Where do we go from here?

We can now answer that question by promising you that, if you have conscientiously followed our suggestions, your personal productivity will increase dramatically, enabling you to handle your job with greater ease, accept greater responsibilities, and still have time to develop and enjoy a rewarding personal life.

And that won't be such a bad return for the short time you have spent reading and working on this book, will it?

Points to remember

1. Productivity and objectives are linked – you can't have one without the other.
2. Completing a personal productivity audit from time to time will help to keep your list of objectives current.
3. Measurable objectives can be written as critical results (CRs) and processed into an action plan.
4. Each activity necessary to achieve the CR must be timed and given a definite priority for action.
5. You should review your plan regularly and change it when necessary.

Index

activities 45
AIDA 66
allocation of work 56
arousing interest 68
asking for action 69
assessment of personal
   productivity 9
associations 93
attributes 91

bar chart 46
body language 71
budgeting
   fixed-base 98
   zero-base 99

committed time 26
communicating 64
commuting 49
completed staff work 60
creative listening 71
critical results 45, 61, 109

decision-making meetings 73
delegation 56
detail 69
discretionary time 26
disorganisation 31, 53

efficiency 19

family time 50
flexitime 49

gaining attention 67

helping meetings work 75
hi-intrusion 37, 77, 78, 80, 81

idle time 26, 28, 47
information meetings 73

job objective 60

leisure time 50
line-loss 73
listening 70
management by objective 60
meetings 36, 72
   casual 78
   routine 77
   special 78

misapplication 38
miscommunication 34, 64
money 96
4 Ms 19, 22

networking 93
non-objectives 29
no-plans 30

objectives 13, 20, 45
   setting 42
organising 53

Parkinson's Law 33
personal attributes 22
   development 92
   objectives 13, 14
   productivity 9, 19, 108
   resources 90
   time 26, 47
planned delegation 57, 58
planning 44
productive meetings 74
   time 26
productivity
   definition 16
   examples 17
   factors 19
   measuring 20
   money 18
progress-stoppers 29

quality 55, 83

resources 19, 22, 110
4 Rights 55

self-assessment 87
standards 58, 59, 61
statutory meetings 74

team-building meetings 73
telephone intrusions 82
time 22
   log 40
   management 25
   wasted 26, 29
travelling 49

utilisation 19, 87
   of machinery 89
   of materials 87